Ren Zhongyi: Frontline Fighter and Economic Reformer

Published by
ACA Publishing Ltd.
University House
11-13 Lower Grosvenor Place,
London SW1W 0EX, UK
Tel: +44 (0)20 7834 7676
Fax: +44 (0)20 7973 0076
E-mail: info@alaincharlesasia.com
Web: www.alaincharlesasia.com
Beijing Office
Tel: +86(0)10 8472 1250
Fax: +86(0)10 5885 0639

Author: Li Ciyan
Editors: David Lammie and Martin Savery
Translator: Jiang Lin
Cover art: Daniel Li

Published by ACA Publishing Ltd in association
with the People's Publishing House

© 2014, by People's Publishing House, Beijing, China
ALL RIGHTS RESERVED. NO PART OF THIS
PUBLICATION MAY BE REPRODUCED IN MATERIAL FORM,
BY ANY MEANS, WHETHER GRAPHIC,
ELECTRONIC, MECHANICAL OR OTHER, INCLUDING
PHOTOCOPYING OR INFORMATION STORAGE, IN WHOLE OR IN PART, AND
MAY NOT BE USED TO PREPARE
OTHER PUBLICATIONS WITHOUT WRITTEN
PERMISSION FROM THE PUBLISHER.

The greatest care has been taken to ensure accuracy but the
publisher can accept no responsibility for errors or omissions, or
for any liability occasioned by relying on its content.

ISBN 978-1-910760-07-9

A catalogue record for *Ren Zhongyi: Frontline Fighter and Economic Reformer*
is available from the National Bibliographic Service of the British Library.

Glossary of Terms

CMC	**Central Military Commission**
CPC	**Communist Party of China**
CPG	**central people's government**
CPPCC	**Chinese people's political consultative conference**
KMT	**Kuomintang (Nationalist Party)**
NGO	**non-government organisation**
NPC	**national people's congress**
PLA	**People's Liberation Army**
PRC	**People's Republic of China**
SEZ	**special economic zone**
SOE	**state-owned enterprise**
SDPC	**state development planning commission**
SPC	**state planning commission**
TCM	**traditional Chinese medicine**

Democratic figures/personages refer to people of note who are 'members of non-CPC political parties'

Preface

The reform and opening up of China ushered in the socialist road with Chinese characteristics and sparked the dawn of a new era. The immortal and meritorious services of Deng Xiaoping, the initiator, chief designer and commander-in-chief of that road, will be eternally engraved on the minds of the Chinese people. He accomplished these outstanding feats with his selfless comrades-in-arms and senior army generals blazing a trail, and going through fire and water with him. The founding fathers and commanders-in-chief of the reform and opening up prompted hundreds of millions of Chinese people to embark together on the new journey that we are still following today. Their eminent contributions deserve to be documented and their deeds should be remembered and admired. They are the role models and examples for the broad masses of party members and cadres to follow on the new journey of reform and opening up.

To cherish the memory of these founding fathers of reform and opening up and to enable readers, especially party members and cadres, to know them better and to learn from them as role models, we decided to publish the *Pictorial Biographies of the Founding Fathers of China's Reform and Opening Up* series. To present these books to readers at the earliest opportunity, we will publish this series volume by volume as each book is completed.

China has entered a new era of reform and opening up. The party central committee with comrade Xi Jinping as general secretary has declared the epoch-making new manifesto of reform and opening up. The implementation of the manifesto requires the devotion and joint efforts of brave generals keeping pace with the times, losing no time moving ahead, fearing no upheavals, abolishing outdated laws and regulations, and defying the negative statements of others; it requires innumerable cadres hurling themselves into the reform and opening-up process; and it requires the collective efforts of hundreds of millions of people. Only in this way can our great cause keep on advancing!

People's Publishing House, August 2014

Alain Charles Asia (ACA) Publishing Ltd is delighted to be associated with the People's Publishing House to bring this book to an English-speaking readership.

ACA, formerly known as ACP (Alain Charles Publishing) Ltd Beijing, was founded in October 1989 and was the first foreign-owned publishing company to be allowed to open an office in China.

In 2007, ACP Beijing was renamed ACA Publishing Ltd to better reflect its focus on China and the Asia-Pacific region. The company specialises in publishing books about China for international readers and has offices in Beijing and London.

ACA Publishing Ltd, October 2016

Contents

Chapter 1	Losing Mother in Childhood and Showing Lifetime Filial Respect for His Stepmother	1
Chapter 2	Deeply Influenced by Patriotic Educator Ma Qianli	11
Chapter 3	Vows with Classmate and Friend Yang Yichen to Expel Japanese Invaders	17
Chapter 4	'December 9' Demonstration and Fight with Military Guards	23
Chapter 5	Boycotting Classes and Moving a Big Bell on a 'Snowy February Day'	35
Chapter 6	Assuming the Heavy Burden of University of China Party Branch Secretary	40
Chapter 7	Disguised as a Couple and Falling in Love	48
Chapter 8	Running Anti-Japanese Cadre Schools While Fighting in Shandong and Hebei	58
Chapter 9	The Couple Shed Blood in Fight against 'Iron Defence Encirclement'	69
Chapter 10	Firmly Resisting the 'Leftist' 'Salvation Movement'	78
Chapter 11	The First Mayor of Xingtai People's Government	85
Chapter 12	Branded as a 'Rightist' and Transferred from Lüda town	90
Chapter 13	Helping Establish the 'Bright Pearls' of the Republic	101
Chapter 14	The First Person to Light up Harbin's Ice Lantern Festival	117
Chapter 15	Amid Chaos, the 'Criticism and Struggle Endurance Champion'	128
Chapter 16	Couple Share Good Times and Bad, and Find Liberation in Cadre School	138
Chapter 17	Taking the Lead in the Debate on the Truth Criterion	147

Chapter 18 Refuting 'Two Whatevers' at CPC Central Committee Conference..................159

Chapter 19 Unswervingly Rehabilitating Wrongfully Accused Zhang Zhixin..168

Chapter 20 Not Turning Pale at the Mention of Prosperity and Talking about Becoming Rich..................181

Chapter 21 Received by Nine Central Leaders Before Governing Guangdong..193

Chapter 22 Proposing 'Three Let Go More' in National Economic Adjustment..205

Chapter 23 Cracking Down on Smuggling and Twice Ordered to Beijing...216

Chapter 24 'Three Unswervinglys' Policy Sustains Guangdong Reform and Opening Up..................226

Chapter 25 Withstanding Pressure to Formalise Support for the SEZs...236

Chapter 26 'Giving Life' to Yuan Geng and Shekou Industrial Park......250

Chapter 27 'Eliminate Corruption, Not Outside Influences' to Solve TV Aerials Problem..................257

Chapter 28 Invited by Henry Fok to Attend a Banquet at the White Swan Hotel..................269

Chapter 29 Supporting Rural Hired-Labour Contracts in Specialised Households..................276

Chapter 30 Guangdong Becomes National 'Pacesetter' of Reform and Opening Up..................286

Chapter 31 Performing Official Duties Honestly and Never Giving Personal Favours..................301

Epilogue..................314

Chronology of Ren Zhongyi's Life..................317

Notes..................334

Chapter 1

Losing Mother in Childhood and Showing Lifetime Filial Respect for His Stepmother

On 20 September 1914, the autumn sky was clear and the air was crisp in south Hebei province. The bright sun was shining and a vast expanse of grass in the green fields swayed in the autumn wind. It was on this day that Ren Zhongyi was born in Xixiaozhuang village in Liyuantun town, Weixian county, Hebei province (Liyuantun was under the jurisdiction of Guanxian county, Shandong province before 1940).

A courtyard of the ancestral home where Ren Zhongyi was born in Xixiaozhuang village in Liyuantun town, Weixian county, Hebei province

The room where Ren Zhongyi was born

Ren Zhongyi's father, Ren Yanfo, formerly called Ren Yongchang, was a man of letters and widely known to have a flair for writing. Busy with teaching Chinese and English in Shandong provincial middle school, he seldom returned home. He married a girl surnamed Ma, who gave birth to a baby girl and then a son six years later. He was overwhelmed with joy and excitement.

An erudite scholar, Ren Yanfo racked his brains to come up with an appropriate name for his son. Clapping his hands, he decided to call him Ren Lanjia, with 'Lan' being his formal family generational name. Since his son was born in the year of Jiayin (the 51st year in the 60-year Chinese calendar) and he expected his son to become eminent and talented in many fields, he named his son with the character 'Jia' (meaning No.1 in Chinese). He was known as Ren Lanjia until he went to university; after graduation, and in order to protect his identity having joined the communists, he was required by the party to change his name to Ren Yi and hurled himself into the War of Resistance against Japanese Aggression. He became Ren Zhongyi after victory in the anti-Japanese war, and he was known by this name for the rest of his life.

Ren Yanfo was a man of letters who taught Chinese in Shandong provincial middle school

When Ren Lanjia was more than two years old, his mother gave birth to his younger sister, Yurong. By nature both cute and clever, Ren Lanjia clung to his parents and got along fairly well with his siblings. Intelligent and carefully taught by his father, Ren Lanjia could reel off reams of ancient Chinese prose and verse as a young boy and became the apple of his parents' eyes. With the father earning a meagre teacher's income, the family lived a financially strained but happy life.

In contrast to the tranquil domestic environment, Ren Lanjia spent his childhood during a period of bloody and chaotic fighting between warlords. The south Hebei plain endured years of conflict, exorbitant taxes and levies, corruption, landlord exploitation, and repeated natural disasters such as drought, floods, wind, storms and plagues that made living conditions so difficult. Adversity befell Ren Lanjia at the age of four, when his mother took him to visit relatives far away. Unexpectedly, his mother came down with black fever, a disease transmitted via the bite of an infected sand fly, and she soon died due to a lack of medical services and supplies. Shaking his mother who was lying on a kang (a heatable brick bed), he cried: "Mum, come to life! Your beloved Ren Lanjia is calling you. Can't you hear me?"

No matter how hard he cried in his hoarse voice, his mother could not be wakened. His relatives put his mother's body onto a farm cart, with Ren Lanjia by her side, and the cart was driven to the hometown. During the bumpy ride, Ren Lanjia wept aloud while clasping his mother's cold hands. His eyes became seriously infected, resulting in inflammation and swelling to the extent that he could no longer see anything. At the end of the journey, he could only hear the cries of others: "Son, stop crying. We've arrived home. Get off!" Then, he parted from his blood mother forever.

After a series of setbacks, especially losing his wife and daughter, Ren Yanfo was determined to bring up his son Ren Zhongyi and other daughter Ren Yurong. So he brought Ren Zhongyi to Shandong

Losing Mother in Childhood and Showing Lifetime Filial Respect for His Stepmother

When he took office as deputy mayor of Dalian in early 1947, Ren Zhongyi brought his father and stepmother from Kuomintang-controlled Jinan that was plagued by chaotic fighting, to the liberated Dalian. This photo shows Ren Zhongyi, his father and his stepmother in Dalian

After his father passed away, Ren Zhongyi was concerned about his stepmother living alone in their former residence in Jinan and paid her a special visit there after he attended a meeting in Beijing in 1978. Here, Ren Zhongyi stands at the door to his parents' former residence with many feelings welling up in his mind

Nine-year-old Ren Zhongyi and his younger brother, aged three

Ren Zhongyi poses with his stepmother and his sons Ren Nianqi (far right) and Ren Kening in Dalian, in early 1950. In the same year, his father and stepmother returned to settle in liberated Jinan

Six months later, Ren Lanjia's sister abruptly died in a plague. Lanjia was terrified: "Why did my mother and sister leave me so suddenly? How will my sister and I spend our remaining days?"

Ren Yanfo was also in grief, to the extent that he wished to die. However, the sight of his young son and daughter in tears gave him the courage to stand up to misfortune. "I'll never give the God of Plague the chance to deprive me of these two young lives," he said. "I will brave all hardship in order to bring them up." He brought Lan Jia to the place where he taught in Heze, Shandong province and had no alternative but to entrust his daughter Yurong to the care of his relatives in the hometown.

Ren's stepmother, Han Qimei, living alone in Jinan

To end the nightmare, he married a girl surnamed Han in his hometown and purposefully renamed her 'Qimei', implying 'mutual respect in a marriage and growing old together' simply because he desired to be part of a permanently happy family. Living up to the consideration and thoughtfulness of her husband, Han Qimei showed the utmost care for Ren Lanjia after she moved to Shandong. When Ren Lanjia was six years old, his stepmother gave birth to a boy who was named Lantian by his father. Since 'jia' (甲) is longer than 'tian' (田) in terms of stroke writing, the relative seniority of the boys was evident in their names.

As family life improved and the three children grew up, Ren Yanfo was able to realise his wish to 'show mutual respect in marriage and grow older together' during what were often turbulent years. He and Han Qimei showed mutual respect and concern and did not separate over a period of more than five decades. His wife was always there to accompany him until he passed away.

Ren Zhongyi pays a visit to his stepmother Han Qimei in Jinan in 1978

Losing Mother in Childhood and Showing Lifetime Filial Respect for His Stepmother

Ren Lanjia was well-known as a dutiful son, respectful and submissive to his parents and he never quarrelled with his stepmother. From the initial post-liberation period, he and his wife Wang Xuan sent part of all their monthly salaries to his parents. They also brought up their sons to take good care of the elderly and designated their second son Ren Kening and third son Ren Kelei to post money to their grandparents. Even when their salaries were forcibly withheld and they had just Rmb80 each month as living expenses in the most difficult period of the Cultural Revolution (1966-1976), they would hide this fact from their parents and remit Rmb50 to them monthly while managing to live a hand-to-mouth existence. When Ren Yanfo passed away in 1968, they were locked up in prison. After hearing the news of his death, the couple continued to post Rmb50 to their stepmother each month until she died. They remitted money without fail to their parents for more than three decades.

The 91-year-old Ren Zhongyi returns to his hometown in October 2004 after a gap of six decades and is warmly received by the townspeople

In October 2004, Ren Zhongyi's sons Ren Kening (right) and Ren Kelei returned to their hometown with their father, and are pictured here beside the tombstone of their grandparents

Ren Zhongyi returned to his ancestral home in October 2004 and said emotionally on seeing the family's old furniture: "These are the chairs I sat on when I was young"

Chapter 2

Deeply Influenced by Patriotic Educator Ma Qianli

During the 16 years from 1921 to 1937, Ren Zhongyi attended four schools – Zhili first model primary school, Hebei first provincial middle school, Hebei College of Law and Commerce, and the University of China. The first three were located in Tianjin, which have since been renamed, while the latter was in Beijing and no longer exists.

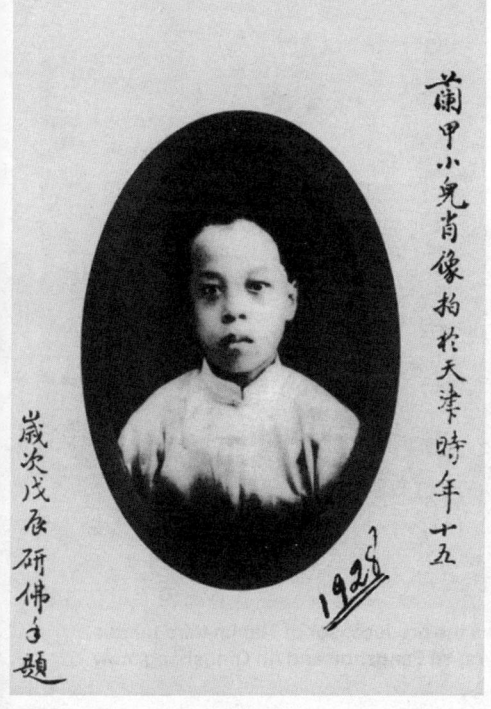

Recalling this photo of himself as a child, Ren Zhongyi said in his later years: "My father's inscription said I was 15 years old. Actually, I was only 14, when I was studying in the middle school. This photo was used when I signed up for the entrance examination to the middle school." He also wrote "1928 7" on the photo, indicating that he was admitted to Hebei first provincial middle school in July 1928

The decision to attend these particular places reflected the wishes of his father, who knew all the good schools in Beijing and Tianjin and wholeheartedly expected his son to receive the best education. Under the guidance of his father, Ren Zhongyi always got excellent exam results in the schools he was admitted to with the approval of his father. The four schools were all famous, featuring good school spirit, qualified teachers and strong academic ethos. What's most important was that the schools boasted vibrant and progressive forces and glorious revolutionary traditions. A large cohort of outstanding teachers and students emerged in terms of both ability and political integrity, and they pursued truth and were devoted to salvaging the motherland with righteous ardour. All these elements had a huge impact on Ren Zhongyi in his formative years.

Hebei first provincial middle school was the predecessor of Tianjin third middle school, where the statues of two martyrs, Yu Fangzhou and An Qingsheng, now stand

Lingdang tower on the campus of Tianjin third middle school

In the autumn of 1928, Ren Zhongyi was admitted to Hebei first provincial middle school, which was well known in Tianjin. Established in 1901, it was Tianjin's first officially run middle school in modern times and was the predecessor of the present Tianjin third middle school. Boasting glorious revolutionary traditions, it witnessed the graduation of two martyrs − Yu Fangzhou, the first chairman of the Communist Party of China (CPC) Tianjin prefectural party committee, and An Qingsheng, leader of the workers' movement. Four of the eight CPC party members admitted by Li Dazhao in Tianjin in 1922 came from Hebei first provincial middle school.

When Ren Zhongyi was admitted, Tianjin's famous patriotic activist and educator, Ma Qianli, acted as headmaster of the first provincial middle school and he exercised huge influence upon him. On moving into the school with his luggage, Headmaster Ma energetically put right school affairs, adjusted and recruited more qualified teachers, implemented the new educational system, adjusted course design, replenished teaching facilities and improved teaching quality. He also organised the building of a sports ground. Every morning, he led the students in a jog around the playground, which improved the school's sports performance to a level that was renowned in Tianjin and even nationwide. In 1902, he set up a football team. The school basketball team participated in the first and second Far Eastern Championship Games on behalf of China and won second place in the second Far East Games. The school also sent its basketball players to participate in the third Far East Games, again representing China. Ren Zhongyi's enthusiasm for sports, especially basketball and football, was formed in the first provincial middle school. His robust body meant he was able to withstand the ordeals and onerous leadership responsibilities in future wars. During the 50 years from the period when he was admitted to the first provincial middle school to 1980, when he took office to administer in Guangdong province, he was not hospitalised even once. Even the cruel torments he endured in the Cultural Revolution could not destroy his body. It was said, with justification, that it was Hebei first provincial middle school that laid a solid foundation for his good health.

Ma Qianli, headmaster of Hebei first provincial middle school

Ren Zhongyi was deeply influenced by the profound atmosphere of patriotic education in the first provincial middle school. Headmaster Ma transformed the school hall into the Sun Yat-sen Memorial Hall, where Ren Zhongyi and his schoolmates would read the testament of Sun Yat-sen in front of a portrait of Premier Sun. Here, under the leadership of Headmaster Ma, they recited two slogans that were hanging on the school hall wall: "Down with Japanese imperialism!" and "Do not forget national humiliation on '9 May 1915'!" Activities were held in the school once a week in memory of Premier Sun, when Headmaster Ma would deliver a speech about carrying on Dr Sun's unfulfilled wishes. When commemorating the day of national humiliation – 9 May 1915, when the Yuan Shih-kai government accepted the humiliating terms of the '21 Demands' – Headmaster Ma would deliver a speech on the stage and urge the students to save the nation from subjugation, ensure its survival and do something useful for society.

In January 1991, Ren Zhongyi inscribed four Chinese characters "我爱母校" (meaning 'I love my Alma Mater') in celebration of the 90th anniversary of the establishment of Tianjin third middle school. The school authorities inscribed the message in gold on a silk banner, which hangs at the front door of the teaching building to educate all future generations

Ren Zhongyi participated in the anti-Japanese demonstration organised by Headmaster Ma and shouted slogans along with the other schoolchildren, such as "Get rid of the unequal treaties" and "Boycott Japanese products". The next day, he and his schoolmates broke and threw away pencils made in Japan and some of them even discarded enamel wash basins made in Japan to express their righteous indignation against Japanese imperialism. On every anniversary of national humiliation, he and his schoolmates would publicise news about these events in the society.

Headmaster Ma also taught his students to develop good living habits, urging them, for example, not to spit on the ground, to take handkerchiefs with them, and to wear clean and tidy school uniforms. The example set by Headmaster Ma in these respects fostered the exalted ambitions of Ren Zhongyi to save the nation and people, and pursue truth; it also informed Ren's good character and morals to get along with people and work seriously.

Headmaster Ma lived and handled school affairs on campus for many years, before suddenly suffering a breakdown from constant overwork and dying from a cerebral haemorrhage. The teachers and students of the school, including Ren Zhongyi, felt extreme sorrow and attended a memorial ceremony held by the Ma family. An unprecedented number of people went to his funeral in Tianjin.

After the Japanese army initiated the premeditated 'September 18' incident[1] in 1931, the incoming headmaster Li Banghan made a speech in the school auditorium on resisting Japan and it was here where Ren Zhongyi and other students signed a petition for national salvation. Ren and other progressive students organised a debating club to relate and discuss the national calamities and corresponding solutions. At that time, the school admitted 38 migrant students from Liaoning province who were studying in the school on a temporary basis. Ren Zhongyi heard from these students from northeast China about the crimes of the Japanese invading army and the deeds of the northeast army of volunteers to withstand the invasion, which further aroused his determination to resist Japanese aggression.

Chapter 3

Vows with Classmate and Friend Yang Yichen to Expel Japanese Invaders

In the autumn of 1931, Ren Zhongyi was admitted to Hebei College of Law and Commerce in Tianjin. Its predecessor was Beiyang Law and Politics Specialised School, the earliest law and politics school in China set up by Yuan Shih-kai in 1906. Founded on glorious revolutionary traditions, the school stood as a flagship for the universities, colleges and middle schools in Tianjin. Li Dazhao[1] was a graduate of the school and he spoke highly of his Alma Mater in a speech celebrating the school's 18th anniversary: "Tianjin functioned as the source of political campaigns in north China, with Beiyang Law and Politics School as the centre. So our school has been playing a vital role in the history of political campaigns in China." After Tianjin was liberated, the school was incorporated into Nankai University.

Students from the former Chinese province of Zhili, including Li Dazhao (middle row, fourth from left), at Beiyang Law and Politics Specialised School (the predecessor of Hebei College of Law and Commerce)

Li Dazhao when he was a student at Beiyang Law and Politics Specialised School

When Ren Zhongyi studied there, the school adopted enlightened management principles and adhered to a fine tradition that promoted academic freedom and all-inclusiveness. In the early 1930s, CPC member and jurist Zhang Youji accepted a teaching appointment at the school. Afterwards, CPC activities began to be held there: Yang Xiufeng, member of the central special agency of the underground CPC in Tianjin, worked as the headmaster's secretary and professor of the department of political science; Nan Hanchen was in charge of the central special agency of the north bureau of the CPC in Tianjin; Wei Jiangong, He Songting, Wen Yongzhi and Lian Yinong were leaders of the anti-Japanese national salvation movement; and underground CPC members in Tianjin taught in the school. With the progressive ideology of the students and a strong political atmosphere permeating all departments, the school was upgraded to be one of the most important places for students in Tianjin to launch the anti-Japanese movement.

Vows with Classmate and Friend Yang Yichen to Expel Japanese Invaders

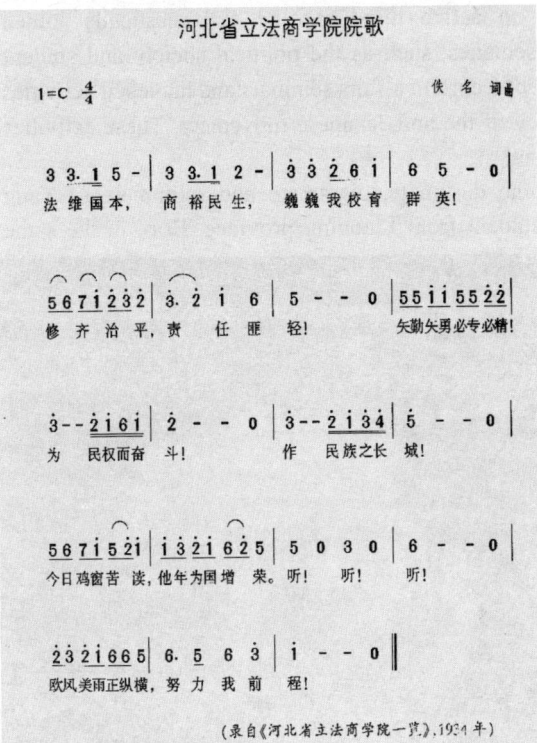

The School Song of Hebei College of Law and Commerce

"The law is the foundation of the nation and commerce promotes people's livelihood,
Our college fosters excellence in law and commerce on a large scale!
To cultivate moral character, govern families and manage the state,
There is no shirking responsibility with diligence, courage, expertise and proficiency.
To fight for civil rights! To be the Great Wall of the whole nation!
Our hard learning from dawn today is aimed at glorifying the nation tomorrow.
Listen! Listen! Listen!
The wind from Europe and the rain from America are swirling around us in all directions,
We should strive hard for a better future."

(From *General Survey of Hebei College of Law and Commerce*, 1934)

Ren Zhongyi had an active mind and he enthusiastically joined progressive students' societies, such as the political society and student council, and participated in current affairs seminars and launched activities to publicise the urgency of the anti-Japanese movement. These activities exposed him to Marxism.

Ren Zhongyi was the deskmate, classmate and roommate of Yang Yichen, a temporary student from Liaoning province. Born in the same

Ren Zhongyi was a classmate and roommate of Yang Yichen, pictured here when he was at the school. They shared the same aspirations and became lifelong friends

Vows with Classmate and Friend Yang Yichen to Expel Japanese Invaders

Ren Zhongyi, front row, third from left

Ren Zhongyi, middle row, third from right

year, they had a common goal and soon became good friends. Originally named Yang Zhenjiu, Yang Yichen was a tall, plain-speaking young man, characteristic of northeasterners. He told his life story to Ren Zhongyi: his father had a good government job and, as the only son of the family, he enjoyed special treatment from his parents. However, on the night of the 'September 18' incident, the Japanese army set up machine guns around the playground of the preparatory upper middle school of Shenyang Fengyong University where he was studying and ordered the school authority to turn in the firearms being used for drills. All the teachers and students, including Yang, were taken as hostages for three days and nights. Cold and hungry, with nothing to eat or drink, most of them broke down and fell onto the ground in the torrential rain. After acquiring the firearms, the Japanese army ordered the students to leave the school that day and to terminate classes. Full of indignation, Yang headed for Beijing alone and planned to join the army of volunteers without even stopping to visit his home. However, his father was insistent that he return home and strenuously persuaded him to continue his studies at Hebei College of Law and Commerce.

On hearing this story, Ren Zhongyi was enraged. "Your hatred is my hatred and even the hatred of the whole nation," he said. "After graduation, we should go and do battle hand in hand and vow to drive out the Japanese devils."

Yang Yichen reached out with both his hands: "Of course!" Fired with indignation, the two hot-blooded young men tightly held their hands together and were inseparable thereafter.

From that moment, they hurled themselves into the torrents of the Chinese revolution and fought shoulder to shoulder as comrades-in-arms for decades. Around 1980, when Ren Zhongyi headed the administration in Guangdong province, Yang Yichen worked as major secretary of the CPC Heilongjiang provincial party committee and later as chief procurator of the supreme people's procuratorate.

Chapter 4

'December 9' Demonstration and Fight with Military Guards

In the autumn of 1934, Ren Zhongyi, Yang Yichen and scores of other graduates of Hebei College of Law and Commerce were admitted to the University of China in Beiping (the Nationalist Party (KMT) name for Beijing). Most of them would later become backbones of the University of China's anti-Japanese national salvation movement. Ren Zhongyi studied in the university's department of political economy, while Yang Yichen was admitted to the department of law.

The gate to the University of China, Beijing

The university was established by Sun Yat-sen in Beijing in the winter of 1912. It was originally known as the Nationalist University before becoming the University of China in the spring of 1917. Li Dazhao and the writer Lu Xun[1] once taught there. The teachers and students of the University of China were at the forefront of struggles against imperialism and feudalism in Beijing, and they trained a large group of revolutionary patriots. As Ren Zhongyi wrote in his memoir in his advanced years: "The University of China was like a liberated area in the war of resistance against Japanese aggression and became a centre of the student movements in Beijing."

Ren Zhongyi enrolled at a time when Marxism was swiftly spreading in the university after the September 18 incident. He often listened to lectures given by a number of communist professors, including Li Da, Wu Chengshi, Yang Xiufeng, Huang Songling, Lü Zhenyu, Cao Jinghua and Qi Yanming. These lectures helped him evolve from a simple patriot to a Marxist.

Led by Dong Yuhua, president of the University of China student union and Beijing student association and a CPC member, Ren Zhongyi threw himself into the anti-Japanese national salvation movement. On 9 December 1935, the students of schools and universities in Beijing held a large-scale demonstration to show their opposition to the establishment of the Hebei-Chahar Political Council,[2] north China autonomy and the Japanese invasion of north China. The demonstration initiated the 'December 9' patriotic anti-Japanese movement that swept the whole country.

At 9am, the gate of the University of China was thrown open and the students rushed out led by Dong Yuhua, general director of the citywide campaign, followed by Ren Zhongyi. The students, braving bitterly cold temperatures of -16C to -17C, headed to Xizhimen in order to meet with their counterparts from Qinghua and Yanjing universities outside the city. However, the authorities closed all the gates. Dong Yuhua decided to avoid an entanglement with the military guards and directly led the procession to Xinhuamen to hand in a petition to the KMT government Beijing branch. Ren Zhongyi and his fellow students broke through the military guard cordon, arrived at Xinhuamen at 10.30am and handed in a petition calling for anti-Japanese democracy to He Yingqin, deputy chairman of the KMT government Beijing branch. However, He Yingqin did not dare come out, deliberately wasted time and dispatched his secretary Hou Cheng to handle the situation. Hou Cheng refused the legitimate demands of the students, mistakenly urged "internal pacification before external resistance" and thereby enraged the students. Student leaders such as Dong Yuhua and Song Li promptly decided to launch a demonstration rather than continue with their petition.

While studying at the University of China, Ren Zhongyi usually returned to see his parents in Jinan during the holidays. This 1935 photo shows Ren outside the front door of his parents' home

On 9 December 1935, school and university students in Beijing held a large-scale 'December 9' patriotic anti-Japanese demonstration. Dong Yuhua led the procession of students from the University of China, followed by Ren Zhongyi. This photo shows students shouting anti-Japanese national salvation movement slogans during the demonstration

Dong Yuhua was a student of the University of China's department of political economy, president of the university's student union and Beijing student association, CPC member and general director of the 'December 9' demonstration citywide. He exerted a huge influence on Ren Zhongyi's journey along the path toward revolution

'December 9' Demonstration and Fight with Military Guards

On the day of the 'December 9' demonstration, Dong Yuhua headed the students in Beijing to Xizhimen and planned to meet with other students outside the city. However, the reactionary authorities closed the gate to prevent students either side of the gate from joining forces

On the morning of 16 December, Ren Zhongyi woke up his dormmate Yang Yichen and his former fellow schoolmates from Hebei College of Law and Commerce in other dorms who failed to participate in the demonstration on 9 December and said: "The Hebei-Chahar Political Council is to be set up today. We will hold a larger demonstration. Are you willing to join us?" Yang Yichen nodded without hesitation. "I'm willing," he said. "I've been anticipating this day for a long time." The other students all conveyed their willingness to join. "Good," said Ren Zhongyi. "You should pretend to stroll along the streets, go out of the school gate in twos and threes to avoid arousing attention and meet at the designated place."

When the procession came to Wangfujing Street, a large number of military guards dispatched by He Yingqin rushed to intercept and beat the unarmed students with broadswords, whips, rifle butts and sticks

Military guards sprayed the students with fire engine hoses before Dong Yuhua took a hose by force and turned it on the military guards

'December 9' Demonstration and Fight with Military Guards

The military guards were prepared to repel the 'December 9' protestors because the reactionary authorities knew about the planned demonstration in advance

Xinhuamen was strictly guarded to prevent the procession from entering Zhongnanhai

The Beijing student association then decided to adopt a diversionary tactic and declared in advance to meet at Tiananmen Square. When a large number of military guards gathered and kept a close watch on the square, more than 10,000 students from all universities arrived at a nearby overpass in four directions and met with citizens to hold a meeting. Ren Zhongyi, Yang Yichen and others led the citizens in shouting slogans such as "Oppose the special treatment of north China", pasting the slogans and distributing leaflets. The rally was held at 11am when more than 30,000 people had already gathered on the overpass square and Huang Jing, one of the people in charge of the headquarters, stood on a trolley bus and gave an impassioned and eloquent speech. Ren Zhongyi deeply felt the great power of the people.

On 16 December 1935, Beijing students held a second demonstration on a greater scale. The procession gathered at the square outside Qianmen square

A demonstration was held after the rally. When the procession came to Xuanwumen, dozens of vehicles stormed into the procession and more than 1,000 military guards rushed forward, beating and whipping the patriotic students with rifle butts and leather belts and carrying out a bloody suppression of the students. Ren Zhongyi, Yang Yichen and others fought with the military guards bare-handed. When night fell, the reactionary authorities extinguished all street lamps and the military guards beat more than 300 students and arrested more than 30 of them. Ren Zhongyi and other progressive students had come to detest the corrupt KMT government and were determined to stick it out and forge ahead with the revolution.

'December 9' Demonstration and Fight with Military Guards

At 11am on 16 December, students and citizens held a rally on the overpass square. Huang Jing, one of the people in charge of the demonstration headquarters, gave a speech from a trolley bus and led the masses in shouting slogans. Here, he is being held by Song Li, one of the student leaders in Beijing

When the procession came to Xuanwumen, more than 1,000 military guards rushed forward and cruelly beat the patriotic students

The procession was bloodily suppressed, more than 300 patriotic students were beaten and more than 30 were arrested by military guards

On 22 December 1935, the Beijing student association held an exhibition of bloodstained garments in the Hall of Sun Yat-sen in the University of China. More than 500 bloodstained garments of wounded and injured students in the 'December 9' and 'December 16' incidents were displayed. The characters 'blood-soaked hard facts' written by Bai Yihua, organiser of the exhibition, were hung on one side of the exhibition room

Bai Yihua was general battalion chief of the anti-Japanese national vanguard, deputy commander of the Northeast United Resistance Army, director of the 10th regiment of the Shanxi-Hebei military region of the Eighth Route Army and deputy commander of the Shanxi-Chahar-Hebei United Resistance Army. He defeated the enemy repeatedly during the war of resistance against Japan, before sacrificing his life for the nation in the vehement fight against the Japanese puppet army on 4 February 1941, at the age of just 29

Bai Yihua's bachelor's degree certificate from the politics department of the University of China

On 22 December 1935, the Beijing student association held a bloodstained garment exhibition in the Hall of Sun Yat-sen in the University of China, where more than 500 bloodstained garments of wounded and injured students in the 'December 9' and 'December 16' incidents were displayed. The exhibition was held by Dong Yuhua and Bai Yihua, who graduated from University of China and was the liaison person and head of the Beijing student association. The exhibition inspired the indignation of patriotic teachers and students, including Ren Zhongyi, and helped rouse the public against the reactionary authorities and reinforced their determination to resist Japan and save the nation.

Chapter 5

Boycotting Classes and Moving a Big Bell on a 'Snowy February Day'

On 21 February 1936, a meeting was convened for all teachers and students in the University of China's Sun Yat-sen Hall where Dong Yuhua, president of the student union, gave a report to summarise the experiences of the student campaigns on 'December 9' and 'December 16' and information about the students in Beijing to publicise the campaigns in the rural and southern areas during the winter holiday.

The University of China's Sun Yat-sen Hall where Dong Yuhua, president of the student union, made a report on 21 February 1936 to summarise the 'December 9' campaign to all teachers and students

When Dong Yuhua was addressing teachers and students, reactionary military guards besieged the University of China, stormed the campus and arrested more than 60 students and a professor. Since it was snowing heavily that day, this came to be known as the 'Snowy February Day' incident

Suddenly, hundreds of armed military guards besieged the University of China, stormed the campus in police vehicles and planned to storm the venue to launch a manhunt under the direction of the school authorities and special agents. Yang Yichen headed a student picket to repel the military guards and warded them off. The military guards brandished batons to drive away the students, who became enraged and grappled desperately with the guards. Tables and chairs were thrown in the confused atmosphere of the Sun Yat-sen Hall. The military guards fired shots to scare the students. Ren Zhongyi and Yang Yichen shielded the student leaders, including Dong Yuhua and Wang Tong, so that they could escape from a side entrance in the chaos. The military guards arrested and took away more than 20 students and one professor. Over the whole night, they took away more than 30 students of Class 14 of the management department and apprehended more than 60 students. The arrested students were beaten with batons and whips by the military guards and put into prison.

Boycotting Classes and Moving a Big Bell on a 'Snowy February Day'

It was a bitterly cold winter day with snow falling from the sky. The University of China students referred to it as the 'Snowy February Day' incident. One arrested student, Liu Tiezhi (Lu Fangming), composed a song to the tune of 'The River All Red' (a poem written by Yue Fei, a famous patriotic general of the Southern Song dynasty). The lyrics went: "The innocents were arrested before the gate of the University of China on a snowy day. All of them were tortured with ropes, shackles and whips. What was their crime? The righteous love for the great motherland! Imprisoned by military guards, they were tormented by strict martial law. Bound by shackles and covered by thin clothes and quilts, they were imprisoned. They were starving with a daily allowance of just two pieces of steamed corn bread and vegetable soup without edible oil. Enraged by the thought of the enemy invaders in the hinterland, they were motivated to fight on!" After it was composed, the song became popular with the students of the University of China and other schools and universities in Beijing.

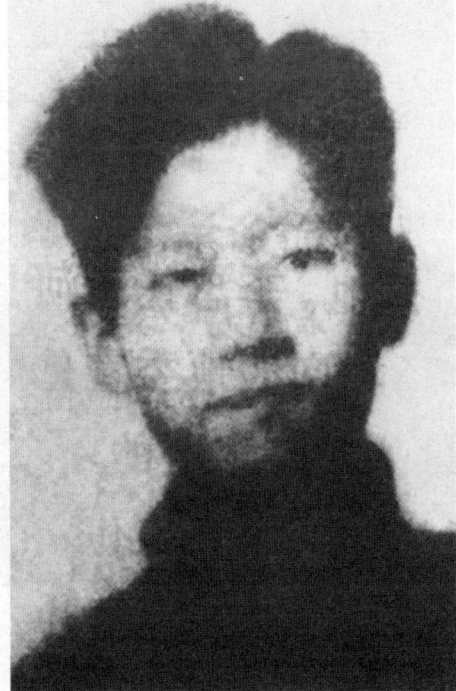

Liu Tiezhi

After the 'Snowy February Day' incident, the University of China was enveloped by white terror. The reactionary authorities clamped down on the Beijing student association and most of those in charge of the University of China student union were arrested. At that time, the school authorities were led by Qi Dapeng, a reactionary director in charge of the university's general affairs, and he ordered a stop to the student campaigns. The students reacted with fury and asked the school authorities why they did not protect the students but instead led the military guards to arrest them. The school authorities ignored their questions. The students were filled with wrath and some of them even choked with sobs. The school authorities acted as if nothing had happened and still ordered the students to attend classes as usual to show that the patriotic students were deserving of punishment. How could the patriotic students be in the right frame of mind to attend classes? At the bell ring for each new class, everyone felt angry.

After the 'Snowy February Day' incident, a sombre atmosphere prevailed over the University of China campus. Although the authorities ordered the university to ring the bell for classes, the students persisted in boycotting lessons and no one studied in the classroom

Boycotting Classes and Moving a Big Bell on a 'Snowy February Day'

On 24 February, Ren Zhongyi quietly asked Yang Yichen: "Let's move the bell away, shall we?"

Yang Yichen slapped his thigh: "Good idea! It shows the unyielding determination of the students. Let's do it right away!"

In the still of night, they quietly went to the bell. Suspended 10 metres above the ground, the bell was firmly attached to the branch of a large tree trunk. It was difficult to move, weighing many kilograms.

Ren Zhongyi stood watch. Tall and with long arms, Yang Yichen managed a kung fu manoeuvre to climb onto the tree, untied the rope fastening the bell, held the large bell in his arms and carried it down with all his strength, inch by inch. Ren Zhongyi came to his aid. They carried the bell to a deep well in the backyard in an effort to throw it down, only to find that the wellhead was sealed up by ice. Unable to throw the bell into the well, they made a detour of more than 150 metres to an artificial hill to the west of the campus. Yang Yichen wormed his way into a cave and hid the bell there.

The next morning the bell did not ring. The teachers and students were puzzled. Some curious students ran to the tree to see what had happened and said cheerfully: "The bell has joined us in boycotting classes!"

Five decades later, Ren Zhongyi wrote down this humorous episode: "The bell became mute and disappeared suddenly. It still remains a mystery to many people!"

In April 1936, with the joint efforts of the party organisation and the progressive teachers and students in Beijing, the students arrested in the 'Snowy February Day' incident managed to get free and were received warmly when they returned to campus.

Chapter 6

Assuming the Heavy Burden of University of China Party Branch Secretary

On 26 February 1936, Li Quan, a student of Beijing Institute of Political Science and Law, went to talk with Ren Zhongyi and asked him whether he was willing to join the Communist Youth League of China. He agreed without hesitation. A few days later, the party organisation approved Ren Zhongyi's membership and appointed him as the party branch secretary of the University of China.

The students' dormitories of the University of China, where Ren Zhongyi effectively carried out secret activities as the university's party branch secretary

Assuming the Heavy Burden of University of China Party Branch Secretary

In March 1936, according to the spirit of the CPC central committee, the north China bureau decided to dissolve the Communist Youth League of China and all former league members were encouraged to become CPC members. In early June, Ren Zhongyi became a CPC member and also the commissar in charge of the party organisation of the University of China.

The article in which Liu Shaoqi criticised closed-doorism and adventurism

In late June 1936, the higher authorities decided to appoint Ren Zhongyi as the university's party branch secretary. At that time, the Japanese army was stepping up its invasion of China, but the KMT government made successive concessions. Beijing was shrouded in the white terror and the CPC lacked strength. The University of China had dispatched many outstanding cadres to work outside the campus. Ren was made responsible for the party's work in the university as a new CPC member at a crucial and difficult moment. However, he was determined to brave the turbulence for the motherland.

Ren Zhongyi twice organised students at the University of China to launch anti-Japanese demonstrations in 1936 in which he persistently implemented the party's guidelines and policies, and laid stress on tactics. The procession proceeded in good order and succeeded

Assuming the Heavy Burden of University of China Party Branch Secretary

He held the view that he could best fulfil his duty by embracing the party's guidelines and policies, and by avoiding 'leftist' and 'rightist' tendencies. At that stage, the whole party, with Ren Zhongyi as an active participant, was rectifying 'leftism'; this laid a solid foundation for his resistance against 'leftist' mistakes in later years. He distributed a copy of *Firing Line* to each party member. This was a confidential party magazine put out by the north China bureau made using a stencil on tissue paper. He also arranged for party members to learn about the rectification of 'leftism' with the emphasis on studying the article written by Liu Shaoqi, secretary of the north China bureau, entitled: *Eliminating the Remnants of the Lisan Line — Closed-doorism and Adventurism*. Strongly opposed to adventurism and closed-doorism, Ren shifted his work to the establishment of the most extensive Chinese united front against Japanese aggression, which topped the agenda of the party branch.

Ren Zhongyi summarised the experience of past student movements. In the 13 June 1936 student demonstration in Beijing against Japan's sending more soldiers to north China, he persistently adhered to the correct guidelines and policies of the party, stringently changed excessively leftist slogans such as 'Oppose the Hebei-Chahar Political Council' and 'Down with Song Zheyuan' applied in previous demonstrations to 'Support Song Zheyuan to firmly resist Japan' and 'Support the 29th army to safeguard north China' as required by the Beijing municipal party committee and the student association. He drew lessons from previous demonstrations and applied partisan withdrawal tactics when the enemy arrived. For example, if military guards blocked them in front, the student procession would reverse direction, thereby leaving the guards far behind. He asked the students to constantly publicise the reasons for resisting Japan and saving the nation to the military guards and persuaded the guards not to act as accomplices of the reactionaries, which produced good results. Some guards were unwilling to beat the students but were ordered by their superiors to drive away the students. They could do little but hug and cry with the students. What a touching scene! Ren Zhongyi also required the students to assemble promptly at a designated place when dispersed. Yang Yichen, chief of the university protection duty team, randomly rolled up banners, hid them under his clothing, displayed them in safe places and mustered the team once again, which helped bring about a successful demonstration.

Ren Zhongyi and some progressive students from the University of China. Front row from left to right: Lü Shixiong, Ren Zhongyi and Guan Datong; back row left to right: Li Chongxun, Yu Xikun, Wang Tuo, Liang Guohua and Yang Yichen

Assuming the Heavy Burden of University of China Party Branch Secretary

Ren Zhongyi often organised underground party backbone groups to discuss the current political situation and work during their activities outside the campus. This photo shows them on a hike to the Old Summer Palace in 1936

In the 1950s, former underground CPC members of the University of China gathered on the banks of the Songhua river, Heilongjiang province, to recall their revolutionary years and sighed with deep emotion. From left to right: Guan Datong, Yang Yichen, Zou Wenxuan and Ren Zhongyi

On 12 December 1936, the Beijing students held another large-scale anti-Japanese demonstration. Before the event, Ren Zhongyi told everyone through the party branch to shout slogans such as 'Celebrate Suiyuan's success in the war of resistance against Japan' and 'All parties and factions unite to resist Japan' and made well-planned and resourceful arrangements for the action. Each party branch would notify their members and the vanguards of national liberation of the action plan the following day. However, they did not gather on campus but met at a designated place after making detours outside to avoid being intercepted by military guards. As a consequence, the demonstration proceeded successfully.

Ren Zhongyi also put significant energy into attracting new party members. Persistently opposing the 'leftist' mistakes of closed-doorism, he seldom considered the class status or family background of applicants but placed emphasis on their personal ideological and behavioural traits when the party branch studied their admission. Taking account of the party's need for absolute secrecy, he clarified that one sponsor was needed for each new party membership. He neither stipulated the probationary period of party members nor demanded any ceremony in an endeavour to uphold the security of the party organisation.

Ren Zhongyi (standing) attends a conference celebrating the 60th anniversary of the December 9 movement in Guangzhou, December 1995

Ren Zhongyi (centre) attends the symposium celebrating the 65th anniversary of the 'December 9' movement, December 2000

As Ren Zhongyi wrote in his memoir about the University of China in his twilight years, when he acted as party branch secretary, the branch had barely more than 10 members. With his unswerving efforts, the number rose to 60-70 within just one year of taking office. This accounted for a fairly large proportion in a university of more than 1,000 students, and was higher than all the other universities in Beijing. He united all university students with the help of these party members and became a standard bearer for the student movement in Beijing. His excellent performance won unanimous accolades from inside and outside the party in the capital.

In late June 1937, Wang De, director of the organisation department of CPC Beijing municipal party committee, notified Ren Zhongyi that the municipal party committee had decided to dispatch him to work as secretary of the CPC Beijing northwest district party committee. He was once again entrusted with a mission at a crucial and difficult moment. He was willing to risk any danger to carry out his duty at a pivotal point in the country's modern history.

Chapter 7

Disguised as a Couple and Falling in Love

In the summer holidays of 1936, to facilitate underground activities, Ren Zhongyi used the assumed name 'Ren Suozhi' and moved to live on the second floor of the west block of Dequan apartments in Taipu street, in the Xidan district of Beijing. The tenants of the apartment were all nonlocal students studying in the city. Ren Zhongyi played the erhu, a two-stringed bowed musical instrument, in the corridor during his spare time.

In April 1986, Ren Zhongyi and Wang Xuan return to the second floor of the west block of Dequan apartments on Taipu street in Xicheng district, Beijing. It was here that they first met each other five decades earlier. Ren lived in the room behind them in this photo

Six female students lived on the first floor of the east block of the apartment. As neighbours, they were often attracted by his erhu playing. They loved singing anti-Japanese songs such as *Graduation* and *Driving the Japanese Back Home*, and especially *On Songhua River*: "From the miserable 18 September, I was forced to leave my hometown due to war and left behind endless treasure.

Wandering! Wandering! I was confined in Shanhai Pass. Wandering…" Their plaintive songs profoundly touched Ren Zhongyi. He knew that they were all students of Northeastern University and exiled from northeast China to study in Shanhai Pass. He noticed that a girl named Wang Jie (formerly Wang Xuan) was particularly special. This vivacious and calm girl, tall and with fair skin, made a favourable impression on him.

One day, Wang Jie found two lines of words written in chalk on the door of their washroom: "Hopefully, you can not only sing songs but also fight on the battlefield with weapons." Wang Jie thought to herself, it might be the young man who played erhu on the opposite side of the apartment block. She found out from the steward that he was called Ren Suozhi.

Ren Zhongyi, Wang Xuan and their son Ren Kelei stand outside Dequan apartments, April 1986. The room behind them is the dormitory where Wang Xuan and other female students of Northeastern University lived 50 years earlier

There was a cinema near Dequan apartments where progressive films were shown on Sunday mornings. Wang Jie and other female students went to the cinema each week. One Sunday morning in the summer holidays, a soviet documentary entitled *Soviet Union Today* was screened. Wang Jie and her friends went to see it. When Stalin appeared on the screen, the students burst out in applause. At that time, the authorities arranged for the cinema to be peppered with military guards for fear that progressive students would be stirred with passion and create a disturbance. Once the cinema emptied after the film ended, Wang Jie and her friends walked back, talking excitedly about the movie. Several boys pushing their bicycles passed them and one of them stopped to chat with Wang Jie. "Wasn't it a good movie?" he asked. Wang Jie saw that it was Ren Suozhi. She had already noticed that he came to see the morning films each week. "Yes, it was good," she replied. He smiled in a friendly manner and jumped back on the bicycle to catch up with his friends.

Soon afterwards, brief notes would appear at the door of the girls' dorm giving details of the time and venue of the next progressive movies. Wang Jie guessed that they came from Ren Suozhi. After that, she found a tightly bound scroll thrown at their dorm. Opening the scroll, she found that it was the progressive periodical, *Immortal*. She believed it was also Ren Suozhi who threw it. One day, she happened to meet him at the dorm door and whispered to him: "Do not throw the periodical. It's too dangerous!" He made no response but from then on no one continued to throw the publication.

On 13 June 1936, Beijing students launched an anti-Japanese demonstration. Wang Jie marched in the front of the procession of Northeastern University that converged with their counterparts from the University of China. The procession was driven away by the batons of military guards. Wang Jie and other girls held hands to form a wall and advanced from the flanks. On that same night, Ren Suozhi went to the girls' dorm and said to Wang Jie: "You girls from the University of China were very brave at the dangerous demonstration today." Wang Jie noticed that he had also participated in the demonstration and was keeping a watchful eye on her.

The cover of *Immortal*, a progressive periodical first published in March 1936

Wang Xuan marched in the front of the procession of students from the Northeastern University in the 'December 9' movement

After the summer holidays, Wang Jie and her colleagues moved to live in the dorm of Northeastern University. She often met Ren Suozhi 'unexpectedly' on campus, not realising that he had actually meticulously planned these encounters.

In November 1936, Wang Jie was admitted to the CPC. This created more opportunities for the two youngsters to get to know each other. In December 1936, Wang De, director of the organisation department of the Beijing municipal party committee, was arrested and put into Beijing prison. The party organisation instructed Ren Zhongyi to participate in the rescue. Disguised as a couple, Ren Zhongyi and Wang Jie visited Wang De in prison pretending to be relatives delivering food, but their main purpose was to pass on information. In January 1937, Wang De was rescued and released from prison. The revolutionary actions of this fictional couple deepened their love for one another.

Disguised as a Couple and Falling in Love

The Lugouqiao (Marco Polo Bridge) incident broke out on 7 July 1937. This photo shows Chinese troops fighting the Japanese army at the head of Lugouqiao

Japanese invaders triumphantly hold a 'city occupation ceremony' in Beijing, 8 August 1937

On 7 July 1937, the Lugouqiao (Marco Polo Bridge) incident broke out and Beijing fell into enemy hands on 29 July. Huang Jing, secretary of CPC Beijing municipal party committee, held an emergency conference and decided that student party members, vanguards and progressive youths should withdraw from Beijing and carry out anti-Japanese campaigns in other parts of the country in a bid to conserve their strength. As required by the municipal party committee, Ren Zhongyi risked his life to stay in Beijing and immediately organised groups of people to evacuate safely from the city. On 10 August, as required by Huang Jing, he headed for Jinan, the largest gathering point for students in exile from Beijing and Tianjin and administered their party membership credentials. Wang Jie worked with him. As required by the organisation, Ren Lanjia (Ren Suozhi) was renamed 'Ren Yi' and Wang Jie as 'Wang Xuan'.

In mid-November 1937, the party organisation assigned Ren Zhongyi a new task to return to Beijing from Jinan immediately and administer the membership credentials of those party members remaining in Beijing. Knowing the task ahead, Wang Xuan proposed that "we'd better dress up as a couple and return to Beijing to lessen the suspicions of the Japanese army". Ren Zhongyi asked Wang De, director of the organisation department of Beijing municipal party committee in Jinan, for instructions. Wang De agreed: "Good, you are a couple." As a consequence, Ren Zhongyi was dressed in a long gown and Wang Xuan in a cheongsam. They disguised themselves as a couple doing business, spoke fluent Japanese that they had learned in school to outsmart the invading troops and arrived in Beijing on a train packed with Japanese.

Ren Zhongyi constantly busied himself with administering the membership credentials of party members in Beijing. One day, he said to Wang Xuan: "Comrade Wang De said we are a couple. It indicates that the party organisation has agreed with our marriage. The Chinese attach importance to the wedding ceremony. Shall we hold our own wedding ceremony?" Wang Xuan responded: "I want a wedding ceremony, too. But how shall we hold it with the bayonets of the Japanese all around?" "We can take a wedding picture under the nose of the enemy. Would that do?" "Good idea!"

Disguised as a Couple and Falling in Love

Ren Zhongyi (left) greets Wang De and his wife in Guangzhou, 1990s

Ren Zhongyi and Wang Xuan attend the celebration of the 65th anniversary of the 'December 9' movement in Guangzhou, December 1995

Ren Zhongyi: Frontline Fighter and Economic Reformer

Wang Xuan happily put on a cheongsam and embroidered shoes. Ren Zhongyi wore a suit borrowed from an underground party member. Unable to find pomade to smooth his hair, Ren used bicycle maintenance grease instead. They held a simple 'wedding ceremony' in a photo studio near Xidan and took their first photo as a couple to capture a love that was kindled in the flames of war. In that year, Ren Zhongyi was 23 and Wang Xuan was 20. From then on, they were never apart during their 70 years of marriage.

In November 1937, Ren Zhongyi and Wang Xuan returned to a Beijing that was under the control of bayonet-wielding Japanese soldiers. Here, at a studio in Xidan, they pose for their first wedding photo. He was 23 and she was 20. They began their 70-year marriage, sharing good times and bad

In the photograph, they did not wear carefree smiles like other newlyweds. Instead, perseverance and composure was etched on their faces and only Ren's red tie gave an indication that this was their wedding day. Outside, Japanese soldiers were patrolling the streets armed with rifles with bayonets.

An individual portrait of Ren Zhongyi, taken in the studio when the couple posed for their wedding photo, shows his courage and determination. Ren knew that a long and bloody war was approaching

Chapter 8

Running Anti-Japanese Cadre Schools While Fighting in Shandong and Hebei

In late 1937, Ren Zhongyi and Wang Xuan left Beijing together and headed for Yan'an in Shaanxi province as scheduled. After they arrived at the Xi'an office of the Eighth Route Army and waited for a couple of days, the organisation notified them to administer party affairs of Shanxi army concerning the Chinese united front against Japanese aggression. "We will willingly do any work, anywhere to resist Japanese aggression," Ren Zhongyi responded.

Former site of the Xi'an office of the Eighth Route Army

In January 1938, Ren Zhongyi took up office as the chief of the organisation section of the political training bureau as well as commissar in charge of organisation of the CPC general party branch of the 66th division of the Shanxi-Suide army. Wang Xuan worked as political assistant of the PLA and CPC party group leader of the Pu county national salvation association of Shanxi province. Although they did not work in the same place, it was not a long distance for them to meet each other.

Anti-Japanese hero Fan Zhuxian, then administrative supervision commissioner and public security commander of the Shandong sixth region, urged the whole country in November 1937 to "pledge their lives not to withdraw south of the Yellow river"

In May 1938, Ren Zhongyi and Wang Xuan were notified by the higher authorities to rush from south Shanxi to Liaocheng, Shandong province to reinforce the backbone of the resistance base in northwest Shandong. They both worked in Liaocheng political cadre school. It was an anti-Japanese cadre school set up by Fan Zhuxian, administrative supervision commissioner and public security commander of the sixth region of Shandong, with the help of the CPC northwest Shandong special committee following the example of Yan'an Anti-Japanese Military and Administrative University, which was known as Shandong sixth region political cadre school. Fan Zhuxian worked as president, CPC member and Professor Zhang Yuguang of Beijing Normal University took charge of overall work as vice president, Ren Zhongyi's teacher Qi Yanming served as academic dean, Ren Zhongyi himself acted as political instructor and member of the CPC general party branch (and later also as secretary of the branch) and Wang Xuan was political instructor, schoolgirl team instructor and commissar in charge of the CPC general party branch. In May 1938, the first cadre school began. A total of four terms of classes were held, with 400 trained and graduating in three months each term. Until Liaocheng fell into enemy hands, the cadre school had trained more than 2,000 cadres for the northwest resistance base.

Anti-Japanese armed forces organised by Fan Zhuxian

Ren Zhongyi gave lectures on dialectical materialism and political economy in the political cadre school. Having no available teaching materials for the political economy course, he created his own in his spare time. Writing each page swiftly in the dim light, he had it transcribed by Wang Xuan. In a short time, he had assembled and delivered the materials for publication. So it was commendable that he was able to compile a set of systematic and complete teaching materials on political economy that were drawn solely from his outstanding memory and solid foundation of professional learning. The teaching materials were printed exquisitely given the prevailing circumstances. Ren Zhongyi's lectures were delivered in an easy-to-understand manner and they were highly popular with the students. Many young students in surrounding areas went to learn in the noted anti-Japanese school in northwest Shandong out of admiration for him.

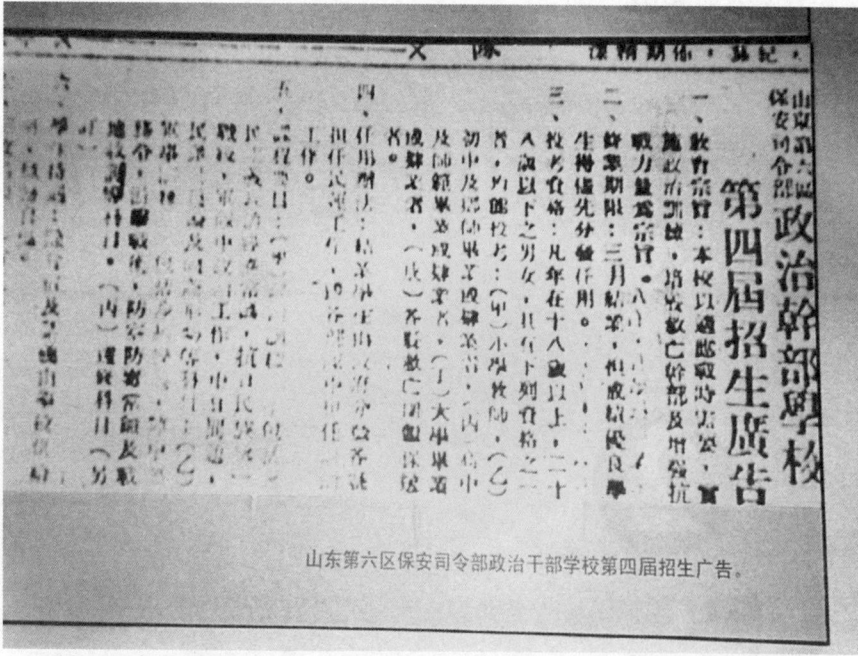

山东第六区保安司令部政治干部学校第四届招生广告。

An advertisement for student recruitment of the political cadre school during the war of resistance against Japan exhibited in Hebei-Shandong-Henan border region revolutionary memorial hall

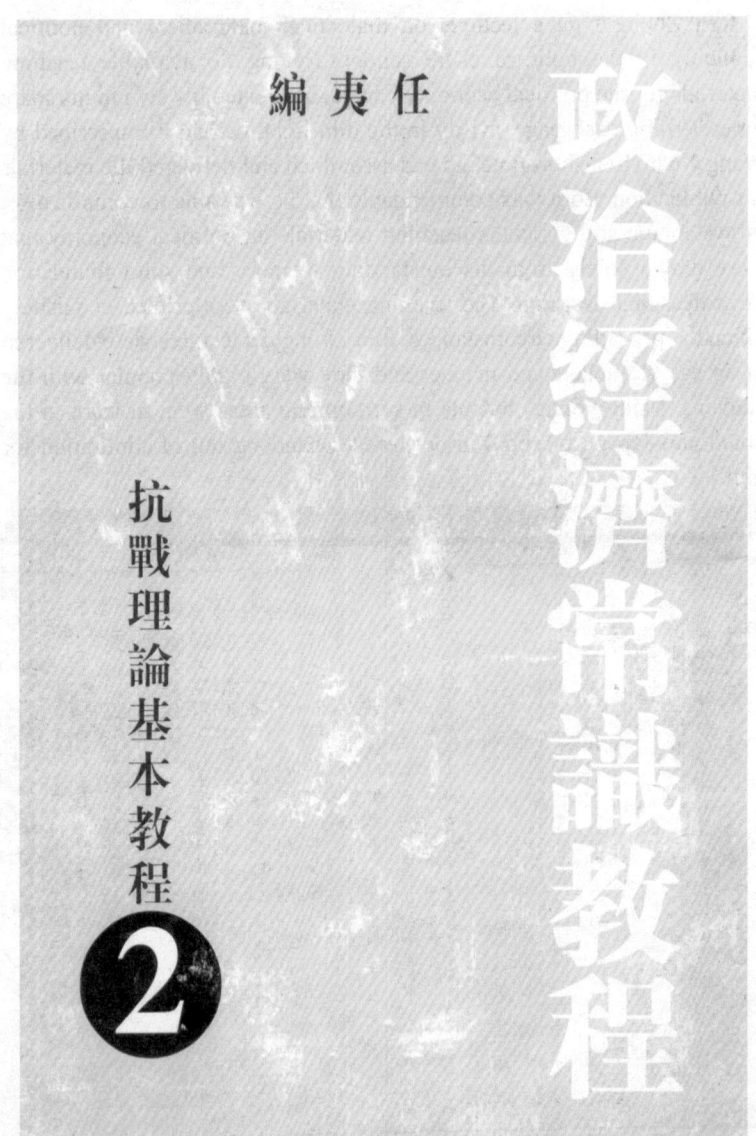

Elementary Political Economics Textbook compiled by Ren Zhongyi (then known as Ren Yi), which he used to train more than 2,000 cadres for the northwest Shandong resistance base

Hebei-Shandong-Henan border region revolutionary memorial hall

Ren Zhongyi had been looking for his *Elementary Political Economics Textbook* without success. Then, on 3 October 2003, on visiting Hebei-Shandong-Henan border region revolutionary memorial hall, he discovered it displayed in the exhibition hall. He also found the magazine *Battlefield Culture* carrying articles written by him and Wang Xuan

Ren Zhongyi stands happily beside the works he compiled in those years, which fulfilled his final wish. He passed away two years later

In October 1938, Ren Zhongyi was appointed secretary general of the headquarters of the third division of the northwest Shandong anti-Japanese guerrilla force. On 14 November, the Japanese army launched attacks on Liaocheng from three directions. Fan Zhuxian instructed Ren Zhongyi, Wang Xuan and other teachers and students of the political cadre school to evacuate safely from Liaocheng, but stayed to defend the city himself. In two days of fierce fighting in the city, Fan Zhuxian, vice president Zhang Yuguang and deputy director of the headquarters' political department and CPC member Yao Dihong, along with more than 700 defending heroes died for their motherland. After Fan Zhuxian was killed, the entire nation mourned deeply. After Liaocheng fell into enemy hands, Ren Zhongyi was dispatched to act as president of the military and administrative cadre school of the sixth branch of the Shandong division of the Eighth Route Army in Taixi on 26 November 1938. The military and administrative cadre school held two classes and trained more than 500 students.

In September 1939, Ren Zhongyi and Wang Xuan were dispatched from Taixi to south Hebei province, which was a vital resistance base behind enemy lines in north China established by the CPC. Ren Zhongyi served as deputy director general of south Hebei administrative education office, deputy director general of south Hebei party committee cadre education office and president of the CPC south Hebei party committee and party school. Wang Xuan was appointed as publicity director of south Hebei women's salvation association and member of the CPC south Hebei women party members' committee.

The former site of south Hebei political cadre school and south Hebei anti-Japanese institute

The party, and administrative and military authorities in south Hebei had always placed importance on training anti-Japanese cadres. After taking office, Ren Zhongyi bravely bore the heavy responsibility, set up two anti-Japanese cadre schools and acted as the president. One was the south Hebei administrative cadre school set up in March 1941 to train the sitting county magistrates, wardens and cadres at departmental and bureau levels. Two sessions were held in all. The other was the south Hebei political school, which began in March 1942 and incorporated the previous school and south Hebei mass movement cadre school. The students there were mostly backbone workers at county and district levels. Again, two sessions were held. The two schools trained a total of 840 cadres from 51 counties in six prefectures in south Hebei in nine months and built a strong and powerful leadership for the people of south Hebei to triumph in the anti-Japanese war. The outstanding working capability and talent of Ren Zhongyi in running the school won the accolade of cadres. It was said in the local area that "Ren (Zhongyi), Wang (Renzhong) and Li (Erzhong) were regarded as the three talents in south Hebei".

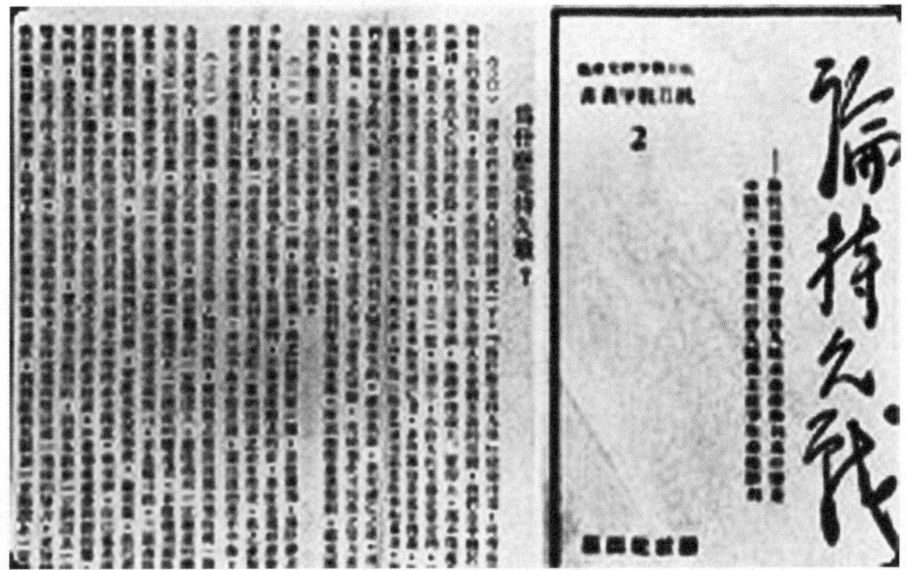

Chairman Mao Zedong's *On Protracted War* served as an important teaching material for students of the cadre school run by Ren Zhongyi

Lively, vivid and characterised by close integration of theory and practice, the two schools run by Ren Zhongyi were popular among cadres in south Hebei. His teaching materials included Chairman Mao Zedong's *On Protracted War*, secretary of northern bureau Yang Shangkun's *Policies for the Resistance Base* and Ren Zhongyi's *Elementary Political Economics Textbook*. The students benefited greatly from the lectures given by the director of south Hebei administrative office, Song Renqiong, on how to overcome difficulties, and the commander of south Hebei military region, Chen Zaidao, on guerrilla tactics.

PLA soldiers in Taihang resistance base

When Ren Zhongyi worked as president of south Hebei administrative cadre school, the anti-Japanese war had reached a point of stalemate. The resistance base suffered difficult conditions. The school had only seven or eight guns with about 10 bullets in each and these would only be enough to breach the enemy's encirclement. For that reason, Ren Zhongyi realised that militarisation was essential for the students to be ready for battle. Each student should take four grenades, a bag of rice and a quilt with them. At the bugle call each morning, they should make their knapsack, have breakfast, attend classes, join discussion and drill with their knapsacks on their backs. At the start, they were not accustomed to this routine. However after a long haul, they felt the method of President Ren was sound and appropriate. On some days they moved to other places, sometimes went out walking for 5km in the night and sometimes fought with the enemy under gunfire. They could start out anytime if they encountered the enemy, attend classes and discussion in safety, and sleep in the camp area with knapsacks on without the need to bother the masses.

The school managed to survive the cruel surprise attacks and mopping-up operations of the Japanese army. Without any fixed site, the students lived in one village one day and then moved to another the next. Many teachers and students were captured or killed in the breakout. To reinforce the strength of school operations, Ren Zhongyi insisted that his wife Wang Xuan transfer to work as director of teaching and discipline as well as teaching full-time in the school. He wrote an anthem to encourage the teachers and students. "We're outstanding children of the Chinese nation," it went. "We left our footprints to the east of the Fuyang river and west of the Weiyun river. Thoroughly trained and persisting in the anti-Japanese war, we are bound to win final victory..."

In a Japanese army mopping-up operation on 29 April 1942, several cadres and students from south Hebei political school were captured and killed by the enemy, and several others were injured. For the sake of safety and with the approval of the administrative office, Ren Zhongyi decided to transfer students from the main campus to their former units; classes on the main campus were suspended, while classes on the branch campus continued until May 1944. He led a rapid march of 11 cadres of the school to Zaobei county, divided into several groups and implemented 'migrant education' in several subareas. He himself was responsible for migrant education in five subareas. In July, he was called back to take office as head of the education department of south Hebei administrative office and party committee cadre education office and continued to take charge of the overall work of the school.

Chapter 9

The Couple Shed Blood in Fight against 'Iron Defence Encirclement'

South Hebei is an area of plains. The period between 1941 and 1943 was the most perilous of the anti-Japanese war, when the enemy deployed the tactics of 'iron defence encirclement' and 'repeated mopping-up operation' and implemented the 'three alls' policy − kill all, burn all and loot all. Fortifications were erected and ravines and gullies criss-crossed the region. The resistance base was divided into many small parts. Ren Zhongyi and his wife could see the enemy fortifications and even hear the discussions of enemy soldiers on the watchtower. They seldom enjoyed an unbroken sleep in the same place. They had to keep on the move − otherwise, they would have faced the risk of encirclement.

During the period when south Hebei fought against the enemy's mopping-up operation, Ren Zhongyi rode on his beloved war horse and broke out of the Japanese army's 'iron defence encirclement'

At dawn on 29 April 1942, with the help of airplanes, tanks, artillery and armoured cars, the enemy launched a four-pronged 'iron defence encirclement' of the south Hebei-west Shandong resistance base. When Ren Zhongyi headed fighters from the administrative cadre school to break out of the encirclement along with battalion troops of the south Hebei party, administrative and military personnel, they encountered low-altitude bombing and strafing by Japanese airplanes. Horses carrying south Hebei bank notes were injured and they bolted, causing the bloodied bank notes to flutter in the air. The resistance fighters were encircled. To reduce casualties, they searched for the weak points in enemy lines for a possible breakout.

Between January and March 1939, the 129th division of the Eighth Route Army and troops in the south Hebei military region jointly repelled the mopping-up operation of the Japanese puppet army in south Hebei and northwest Shandong. The main force of the 129th division later returned to Taihang resistance base and was ready to smash the summer 'mopping-up operation' of the Japanese army in the Taihang mountain area. This photo shows the 129th division marching towards Taihang mountain

The Couple Shed Blood in Fight against 'Iron Defence Encirclement'

On 29 April 1942, the Japanese army in north China abruptly implemented an 'iron defence encirclement' of south Hebei resistance base behind enemy lines, and the south Hebei military region headquarters was encircled. The repeated charges of the only combat forces – the cavalry of the 129th division and the special agent regiment of the headquarters – were suppressed by the sheer firepower and military strength of the Japanese army. The cavalry charged forward at the last minute and broke through, despite suffering heavy casualties, so that the personnel of the main organs and large numbers of soldiers and civilians in the south Hebei military region could break through the encirclement of the Japanese army. This photo shows the bloody aftermath of the cavalry who had come under blanket fire and the tight encirclement of the Japanese army

In the beginning, about 10 people followed Ren Zhongyi and finally only a liaison man with an injured leg stayed with him. Wang Xuan disappeared without trace. Ren asked the liaison man to hide in a nearby village, while he managed to break out of the encirclement after running for three hours. Tired and thirsty, without a drop of water, he found two pails of cold water at the roadside and drank most of it without pause. As evening fell, he arrived at the village of Renzhuang and received an extraordinarily warm welcome. The local residents found him a safe place to stay the night. The next morning, he hastened to the rally point, safe and sound. Seeing Wang Xuan and 20-odd cadres of the cadre school, but realising that other cadres and students had been captured or killed, he felt a mixture of joy and sorrow.

South Hebei bank notes issued by South Hebei Bank were legal tender in circulation and use in the southeastern Shanxi resistance base under the leadership of the CPC and Eighth Route Army and, later, the Shanxi-Hebei-Shandong-Henan border region resistance base of the democratic regime

Wang Xuan had been lying prone in a field of rye when an enemy plane started bombing. After the plane left, she could not recognise anyone, so she ran to a nearby village only to find that it had been outflanked by Japanese puppet army troops. She ran to the courtyard of an oil mill in the village and an old man hid her in some hay meant for cattle. A gang of Japanese soldiers arrived and asked: "Have any eighth route army soldiers come here?" The old man said "No".

The Japanese puppet army then poked around the courtyard with bayonets, coming close to stabbing Wang Xuan several times. Holding her breath and staying still, she could hear the miserable cries of those being killed or injured with bayonets. In the middle of the night, the old man called to her: "Comrade, come out. The Japanese have gone." She saw blood everywhere in the yard now that the dead and wounded had been taken away. The old man treated her to a meal and dispatched another person to escort her from point to point along her journey. The next day she was finally able to return to the troops safely. "I managed to return alive thanks to the support of good people," Wang Xuan said with emotion. "We should remember them forever."

Wang Xuan underwent another alarmingly dangerous experience when she acted as a member of Hengshui county party committee and director of the county anti-Japanese union. At that time, the village she was in was suddenly besieged by the Japanese army and she ran into a household where an old woman hurried to put her hair in a bun, covered her head with a handkerchief, smeared her face with stove ash and asked her to sit silently before the stove. Five or six Japanese rushed in, holding rifles with bayonets, and asked: "Who are you?" The woman lowered her head, said nothing and busied herself with the fireplace bellows. She then said: "She's my daughter-in-law whom my son married when he was doing business outside Shanhai Pass." The Japanese soldiers searched around, found nothing and left. She had managed another narrow escape.

When serving as a member of the standing committee of south Hebei fifth prefectural party committee and commissioner of south Hebei fifth subarea in 1943, Ren Zhongyi energetically motivated soldiers and civilians in the prefecture to engage the enemy in warfare on the plains, in tunnels and by laying landmines. "The tunnels in the south Hebei plain were built as well as those in the middle Hebei plain," he recalled in his twilight years. "I had been besieged by the enemy and strafed by gunfire several times. I rushed out from the tunnels under the protection of local armed forces and soldiers and civilians." This photo shows a scene of tunnel warfare in the middle Hebei plain during this period

Ren Zhongyi organised and joined soldiers and civilians in the area under his administration in destroying enemy strongholds. Here, the PLA cheers for victory after taking a stronghold from the Japanese army

The Couple Shed Blood in Fight against 'Iron Defence Encirclement'

One day in May 1943, Ren Zhongyi, serving as a member of the standing committee of south Hebei fifth prefectural party committee and commissioner of south Hebei fifth subarea, and his wife Wang Xuan experienced the most dangerous encirclement in their lives. They inspected the work in a village and planned to hurry to the administrative office and military subarea of a village in Zaobei county overnight to attend a military subarea meeting the next day. It was extremely late and they followed the advice of the village cadres to stay for a night. As dawn broke the next day, Ren Zhongyi, Wang Xuan and their protectors hurried to the military subarea, hearing the sound of machine gun fire from the south and seeing many people drive cattle and donkeys as they headed northwards. They knew that they had been encircled by the Japanese. With the enemy approaching from the south, they escaped southeastwards, found a gap in the encirclement and broke through by chance. They heard gunshots in the village where they had stayed the night before. After the enemy withdrew their troops at nightfall, they knew that the headquarters of the military subarea was encircled in a waist-deep ditch by the enemy and that the commander and vice commander as well as many cadres and soldiers of the subarea had sacrificed their lives. Although the secretary of the prefectural party committee, Li Erchong, escaped from the encirclement, his left wrist was struck by a bullet. If the group of people headed by Ren Zhongyi had rushed to the military subarea the night before, they would have been besieged in the ditch and might have lost their lives. Later, if they had set out from the village where they stayed overnight, they would also have been besieged and killed. These were highly dangerous times.

Wang Xuan gave birth to their first son in 1939 when the couple were engaged in operations alongside the army day and night on bumpy roads. So they named their first son Ren Qi, because Qi (崎) means 'bumpy' in Chinese. Unable to bring the baby with them, they had to entrust him to the care of Ren Zhongyi's sister, Ren Yurong. In the 1942 famine, Ren Qi and Yurong's own child starved to death. Wang Xuan gave birth to their second son in July 1942, delivering the baby herself on a *kang* belonging to ordinary people. In honour of the dead Ren Qi and the suffering of their second son, they named him Ren Nianqi because 'nian' (念) means 'missing' or 'commemoration' in Chinese. Wang Xuan often went to a sorghum field to escape enemy mopping-up operations with Nianqi in her arms. Before he was one month old, Nianqi was given for safety to a childless rural woman surnamed Duan, who later gave birth to her own child and who then returned Nianqi.

The monument of the '29 April 1942' operation against the enemy's 'mopping-up' campaign in Gucheng county, south Hebei

The Couple Shed Blood in Fight against 'Iron Defence Encirclement'

Ren Zhongyi organised and joined cadre school students along with soldiers and civilians in destroying enemy fortifications

Ren Zhongyi, Wang Xuan and their five-year-old son Ren Nianqi in Dalian, 1947

Chapter 10

Firmly Resisting the 'Leftist' 'Salvation Movement'

The Yan'an rectification campaign began in 1942. It was an unprecedented Marxist progressive education and ideological emancipation movement for the whole party, which elevated Marxism-Leninism in the party and brought about unprecedented unity across the whole party.

Matian town in Zuoquan county of Taihang mountain, where the rectification movement of the north China bureau party school of the CPC central committee was launched, and later the erroneous 'salvation movement' featuring 'forced confessions, whistle-blowing and investigation into 'cadres' archives' occurred

Firmly Resisting the 'Leftist' 'Salvation Movement'

The 'delinquent salvation movement' took place at the same time. In July 1943, Kang Sheng, deputy director of the general study committee and director of the CPC central social department, delivered a mobilisation report at a meeting for cadres in Yan'an, unleashed the so-called 'delinquent salvation movement' during a routine inspection of cadres, took struggles to extremes featuring 'forced confessions, whistle-blowing and investigation into cadres' archives' and produced a huge number of unjust, false and erroneous cases in a matter of just 10 days. The CPC central committee rectified the mistake later. In the spring of 1944, the authorities began to screen and redress the erroneous cases and apologised to those who had been wronged.

Li Erchong, who became secretary of the CPC south Hebei fifth prefectural party committee and political commissar of the south Hebei fifth subarea in November 1943, became the target of 'salvation' in the rectification movement, was tortured to extract confessions and saw his case rectified later

The erroneous 'delinquent salvation movement' affected other resistance bases. In November 1943, Ren Zhongyi, commissioner of south Hebei fifth subarea, and Li Erchong, secretary of the CPC south Hebei fifth prefectural party committee and political commissar of south Hebei fifth subarea, were dispatched to the north China bureau party school of the CPC central committee. Armed with weapons and special protective clothing, they trekked day and night with two guards, and secretly crossed the blockade between Taihang and south Hebei, before arriving in Taiyue.

Soon afterwards, Ren Zhongyi was astonished to receive a telegram from the central committee saying there were many spies in the 'salvation movement' that led to the "accusations at large and small meetings" and "leniency for those who confess and severe punishment for those who resist". More than a month later, Ren Zhongyi and Li Erchong were transferred to study in the rectification movement in the north China bureau party school in Matian, Zuoquan county, Taihang mountain. The cadres, especially intellectuals who had worked in the white area, were the main targets of suspicion and 'salvation'. Li Erchong rapidly became a target and was forced to admit tipping off the Japanese during a mopping-up operation in May. To cover up, he 'broke his own left wrist', was convicted as a 'traitor' and 'enemy spy' and suffered more cruel forced confessions. Unable to bear the torture, he escaped into the mountains and was recaptured for more torture.

Ren Zhongyi was suspicious of the existence of many 'spies' and 'hidden traitors'. He regarded the investigation as subjective, one-sided and ignorant, and deemed it wrong, not to mention inhuman and cruel, to practise 'forced confession, whistle-blowing and investigation into cadres' archives'. Then, unexpectedly, he found himself to be a target of 'salvation'. Investigators pinned two labels on him. First, they said he was a 'KMT spy', claiming he had connections with a KMT special agency when he was secretary of the party committee of the University of China, although no evidence was produced. Second, he was alleged to be part of a 'Trotskyite bandit gang'. They could not cite any 'Trotskyite' words he had used or deeds he had done, and even he himself did not know the theoretical perspectives of Chinese 'Trotskyites'.

Investigators tried to extort confessions from him day and night. They slept in three shifts but did not allow Ren to sleep. They only let him nap for a few minutes each time, totalling no more than several hours in a month. Whenever he did sleep, the investigators would beat him awake, attempting to make him confess to false charges under torture.

When he was at a particularly low physical ebb, the person in charge of the cadre investigation committee came to 'persuade' him to 'confess' to everything. "I hope the party will be prudent, prudent and more prudent," Ren retorted. The person in charge said: "The party demands you to confess, confess and confess more!" Ren replied: "I believe in the party!" The person in charge said: "The party reckons you have problems." He replied: "I believe in Chairman Mao." The person in charge said: "Chairman Mao also reckons you have problems! Do you know where you are?" He answered: "The north China bureau party school." The person in charge uttered, "What party school? It is 'gebiewu'!" 'Gebiewu' (格别乌) was the transliteration of the Russian abbreviation for the State Political Security Bureau of the Soviet secret service and was later renamed the Soviet State Security Committee or KGB, transliterated as 'kegebo' (克格勃).

On hearing the sentence, Ren Zhongyi felt astonished and his head was bursting with dark thoughts.

The cadre investigator found Wang Xuan, who was participating in the rectification movement in the Taihang bureau's Pingyuan branch in the role of study group leader, and asked her to confirm a spurious 'confession by Ren Zhongyi'. Wang Xuan felt it was fabricated and categorically denied it. The investigators later produced a so-called 'testimony of Wang Xuan' and attempted to fool Ren Zhongyi into confession. At the sight of his wife's testimony, Ren Zhongyi shouted furiously: "You're talking rubbish! It's impossible!" thereby frustrating the attempted conspiracy of the interrogators.

Tortured, dangerously ill and in a trance, Ren Zhongyi became aware that, if things continued in this manner, he would fall into a confused state of mind, be forced to confess what they wanted and be labelled as a 'spy' and 'Trotskyite bandit'; then, not only would he acquire a notorious reputation and be seen as a hostile element who betrayed the party and the people, but he would also lose his life. He knew that some good comrades had been executed dubiously in the 'salvation movement' and he would be powerless to remove the stigma from his name. No, he would not await his fate. He was determined to keep a clear mind and hold his ground.

Therefore, whenever he nodded off, he secretly pinched his thigh to stay awake. If he could not endure it any more, he would bite his lips and tongue, to the extent that his tongue bled. He was determined never to make any confession even if it involved biting off his tongue.

The three-month interrogation could not extort a confession from Ren Zhongyi. And the interrogators gave up and kept him under house arrest for as long as eight months. Labelled as a suspicious 'Trotskyite bandit', he was transferred by the leaders of the north China bureau to be deputy editor-in-chief of Xinhua bookstore. In reality, he was not tasked with any editing work, so he volunteered to do some proofreading over a period of several months. He once lived with Zhao Shuli, author of *Peasant Takes a Wife*, sleeping on a heated *kang* in a shared thatched room. He then moved to a single room in a farmer's house. One cold night, he fainted due to the gas emissions from a coal stove. Luckily, he lay near a door and was able to breathe some fresh air and regain consciousness.

In the room, he read many books on Marxism and Leninism, wrote a candid diary for a couple of months and noted down the faults in the 'salvation movement' in Romanised Chinese that he learnt in the University of China so as to keep his thoughts secret. The palm-sized diary was bound in scrap paper, meaning that it was both portable and easily hidden. He wrote a poem called *Song of Zhang River*, which began and ended with the following lines: "The Zhang river is clear / from water surface to river bottom / limpid and transparent." He compared the Zhang river flowing past the party school to his own history without any guilt. It was heartbreaking that this diary, which accompanied him for more than 20 years, was burnt to avoid implication in the literary inquisition during the Cultural Revolution.

The whole 'salvation movement' labelled many outstanding party cadres as 'spies' and 'Trotskyite bandits', which aroused the intense indignation of party members and cadres who clamoured their disapproval to the central committee. Mao Zedong was apprehensive of the tendency of investigators to expand the campaign to 'eliminate counterrevolutionaries' and publicly apologised to the victims on many occasions. In 1944, the CPC central committee gave instructions to rectify the mistakes of the 'salvation movement' and correct the unjust, false and erroneous cases. The

Firmly Resisting the 'Leftist' 'Salvation Movement'

'salvation movement' of the north China bureau party school that shocked north China did not 'salvage' a single 'spy' or 'Trotskyite bandit'. In the end, all victims won political rehabilitation. In April 1945, Ren Zhongyi resumed his work after staying in the north China bureau party school for 18 months and acted as a member of the standing committee of the CPC south Hebei second prefectural party committee and commissioner of the south Hebei second prefectural commissioner's office.

In April 1945, Ren Zhongyi (centre) was proved innocent and resumed his work after staying in the Taihang mountain north China bureau party school for 18 months as the target of 'salvation'

Recollecting the unforgettable 'leftist' disaster in his later years, Ren Zhongyi said: "I didn't expect Chairman Mao to bow in apology to all the 'salvaged' innocent at the meeting in Yan'an. It showed the open mind of a great leader and the spirit of a Marxist seeking truth from facts. It is a pity that the historical lesson was not carefully drawn and turned to valuable experience." He then commented on the actions of the person in charge: "It could be said that there was a 'red terror' in the atmosphere in those days. No one stood up to resist it then. The comrade in charge was no exception."

The person in charge felt bitterly remorseful and guilty in his old age, with his soul often severely tormented. "In 1944, I hurt some comrades in the rectification campaign of the north China bureau party school," he said. "Thinking about it now, I am still weighed down." "Summarising the experiences and lessons, I wrote down two things on my mind, 'loyal stupidity and stupid loyalty'."

Chapter 11

The First Mayor of Xingtai People's Government

Japan delivered an official note to China, the US, Britain and the Soviet Union respectively on 14 August 1945 in which it accepted the *Potsdam Proclamation*. On the following day, Japanese Emperor Hirohito broadcast a radio message entitled the *Imperial Rescript* and declared that the public should accept the proclamation and surrender unconditionally. Jubilation erupted everywhere in south Hebei, and Ren Zhongyi and the soldiers and civilians of the region all felt proud and elated.

The battle to liberate Xingtai erupted on the night of 23 September 1945. The south Hebei second subarea troops braved a shower of bullets and captured the eastern wall of Xingtai on the morning of 24 September

Nevertheless, the KMT peace preservation corps took the opportunity of the Japanese army's evacuation to occupy Xingtai in an attempt to become firmly entrenched in the city in advance of a takeover by the large KMT forces. Xingtai had always been a strategic town in south Hebei, being a north-south traffic hub and a vital tactical stronghold on the Beijing-Hankou railway. In response to a plot by KMT reactionaries to advance northwards and launch attacks on the liberated area along the Beijing-Hankou railway, the Shanxi-Hebei-Shandong-Henan military region decided to block the enemy and capture Xingtai.

The Taihang sixth subarea troops erect scaling ladders to attack the city in the battle to liberate Xingtai

On the night of 23 September, troops of the Taihang first and sixth subareas and south Hebei second and fourth subareas jointly launched vehement attacks on Xingtai from all directions. As a member of the standing committee of south Hebei second subarea and commissioner of the second prefectural commissioner's office, Ren Zhongyi collaborated with the troops and arranged for militias and migrant labourers to join the battle. After a fierce confrontation, they secured victory on the morning of 24 September. All the defending enemy troops, apart from a few who escaped, were killed and more than 3,000 officers and men of the puppet army were captured. The liberation of Xingtai was a strategic success for the PLA, connecting the liberated area in south Hebei and Taihang, and cutting off the route of Chiang Kai-shek's army to advance northwards in its bid to secure victory. This significant battlefield success paved the way for the Beijing-Hankou railway battle.

After the battle, soldiers pose on the walls of Xingtai, hailing the city's liberation

The military control commission issued a general order to all citizens of Xingtai on 25 September, declaring the establishment of the CPC Xingtai municipal party committee and Xingtai municipal government, with Ren Zhongyi as first secretary of the municipal party committee and first mayor of the municipal government. People from all walks of life sang and danced in the streets to celebrate the liberation of Xingtai

The people of Xingtai celebrated their liberation, with red flags flying on the Qingfeng tower and the whole city resounding with cheers. Citizens managed to cut, dye and sew red flags to show their support for the victory.

On 25 September, the military control commission issued a general order to all citizens of Xingtai. Posted in high streets and back lanes, the order declared the establishment of the CPC Xingtai municipal party committee and Xingtai municipal people's government, with Ren Zhongyi as first secretary of the party committee and first mayor of the municipal government. Xingtai was the first liberated prefecture across China following victory in the anti-Japanese war and Ren Zhongyi was one of the first mayors to be appointed since the war of liberation. Just 42 days later, the Japanese army declared their surrender.

The First Mayor of Xingtai People's Government

After taking office, Ren Zhongyi immediately initiated support for the frontline of the national war of liberation. Here, local people put on a spectacular display to show their support for the frontline after the liberation of Xingtai

Chapter 12

Branded as a 'Rightist' and Transferred from Lüda town

In October 1945, the higher authorities issued an emergency order: the central committee required a large number of cadres and troops to be rapidly transferred from Yan'an and all liberated areas to northeast China to establish a consolidated resistance base. The north China bureau transferred 100 members and five regiments of cadres from south Hebei administrative office and Taihang first subarea to march to northeast China. Ren Zhongyi and Wang Xuan were both on the list. Therefore, Ren Zhongyi, who by now had dropped the name 'Ren Yi' as required by the organisation, set out with his wife Wang Xuan and his two-year-old son Ren Nianqi. In January 1946, they arrived in northeast China. They were not to return to the Shanhaiguan

Ren Zhongyi (second from left) and colleagues when he served as deputy mayor and deputy commissioner of Fushun in January 1946

pass for another 35 years. Wang Xuan stopped off in her hometown of Fushun only to discover that her mother had died eight years previously. She realised that her mother had lost her life in the chaos caused by war and that the family home had been razed to the ground.

Ren Zhongyi in March 1946, when he was a member of the CPC Yingkou, Dandong and Dalian prefectural party committees, and deputy commissioner and party committee secretary of the commissioner's offices of the three prefectures

Ren Zhongyi when he was deputy mayor of Dalian and Wang Xuan as chair of northeast China women's federation in November 1946

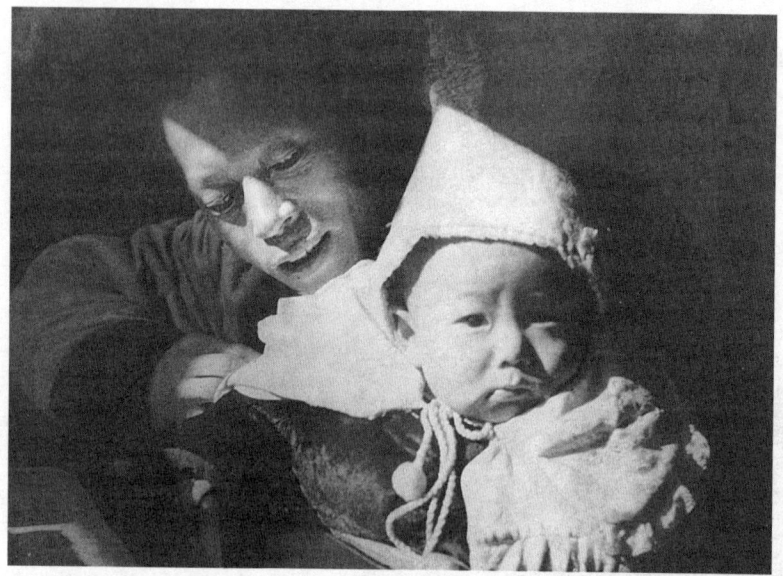

The joy at the arrival of their second son in 1946 dispelled a lingering sorrow in the lives of Ren Zhongyi and his wife. Ren Zhongyi shows tender care for his robust child

From 1946 to 1951, Ren Zhongyi held the following positions: deputy mayor and deputy commissioner of Fushun; member of the standing committee and deputy commissioner of CPC Yingkou, Dandong and Dalian prefectural party committees; secretary of the party committee of the commissioner's offices in these three prefectures; deputy mayor of Dalian; deputy secretary of Dalian municipal party committee; secretary of the party committee of Dalian municipal government; secretary general of northeast China government office and Lüda (now incorporated into Dalian city) prefectural administrative office and deputy secretary of the party committee; director of Lüda district committee clerical office; member and secretary general of Lüda municipal party committee and secretary of the youth working group of Lüda municipal party committee; and secretary of the communist youth league of Lüda municipal party committee. Wang Xuan served as: director of teaching and discipline, and member of the general branch of Lüda Jianguo college; chair of northeast China women's federation; secretary of the women's work committee of Lüda prefectural party committee; deputy director of the civil affairs department of Lüda administrative office; director and deputy secretary of the party committee of Lüda civil affairs bureau; director of Lüda personnel bureau; and secretary of the party membership committee of the municipal government.

When they worked in Lüda, Ren Zhongyi and Wang Xuan enjoyed a peaceful environment without war for the first time in their married life. They injected enormous zest in consolidating the new democratic regime, working both day and night. Although extremely tired, they felt entirely free from worry.

Ren Zhongyi and his eldest son at Dalian municipal government gate, 1947

Nevertheless, they feared they would be unable to combine their busy working lives with an expanding family, as two more sons arrived in quick succession. When Wang Xuan was pregnant in 1946, they were anxious because they were working round the clock and were intellectually embroiled in political affairs. Besides, they had to take care of their eldest son Nianqi, who had just started primary school. Although they deeply loved their unborn child, they feared that they could not take good care of him and thereby might harm his growth. Consequently, Wang Xuan took the painful decision to abort the child by consuming a large quantity of quinine. Unexpectedly, a robust baby came into the world, safe and sound. Feeling both surprise and joy, they named him Kening, meaning 'invincible nemesis of quinine in the womb, full of vigour and vitality'.

Wang Xuan lovingly holds her third son Kelei

Branded as a 'Rightist' and Transferred from Lüda town

Ren Zhongyi when he was deputy mayor of Dalian and deputy head of Xigang district of Dalian, 1947

Ren Zhongyi (fourth from left) sees off his comrades-in-arms in Dalian before they march southwards to liberate the country, 1947

Ren Zhongyi (second from left) as secretary general of the northeast China government office and Han Guang (fifth from left) as chairman of the office, October 1948

Ren Zhongyi reviews a parade in his capacity as secretary general of Lüda (Dalian) prefectural administrative office and deputy secretary of the party committee, 1949

Their third son was born in 1950 when Ren Zhongyi was busy working as secretary general of Lüda (Dalian) prefectural administrative office and director of Lüda district committee clerical office. Wang Xuan was also very busy with her duties as director of Lüda personnel bureau and vice president of the newly established Lüda administrative cadre school, where Mayor Han Guang was president. They were already looking after two children at this point, and another child was bound to be an additional burden. However, the baby arrived tenaciously and his parents held their lively son lovingly and with happiness. So they named him Leilei, which sounds the same as the word 'tired' in Chinese. Here was another tough boy. When Leilei was studying in higher primary school, his name was changed to Kelei, which matched up with Kening, the name of his second older brother. Kelei means 'winning with unshakable self-control' or, more literally, overcoming or resisting tiredness.

Ouyang Qin, when he was first secretary of Lüda municipal party committee

When he served as secretary general of Lüda (Dalian) prefectural administrative office and Lüda municipal party committee, Ren Zhongyi often proposed to the leaders and cadres of the administrative office and the municipal party committee that political campaigns should be initiated on the basis of inspection, research and seeking truth from facts. He also advocated laying emphasis on evidence, especially physical evidence, rather than readily believing oral confessions, and to avoid forced confessions, corporal punishment, threats and intimidation. His suggestions won the total support of Ouyang Qin, first secretary of Lüda municipal party committee and Hu Zhonghai, the cadre in charge and minister of the organisation department in charge of discipline inspection.

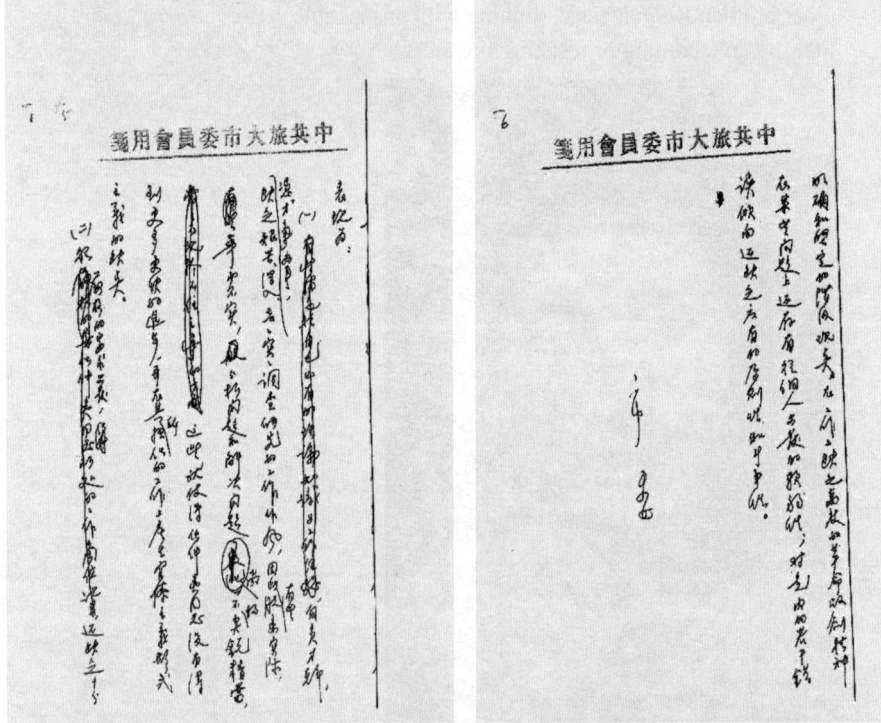

Before leaving Lüda (Dalian), Ren Zhongyi regarded himself as "basically correct in understanding and persistent in implementing the party's policies and guidance"

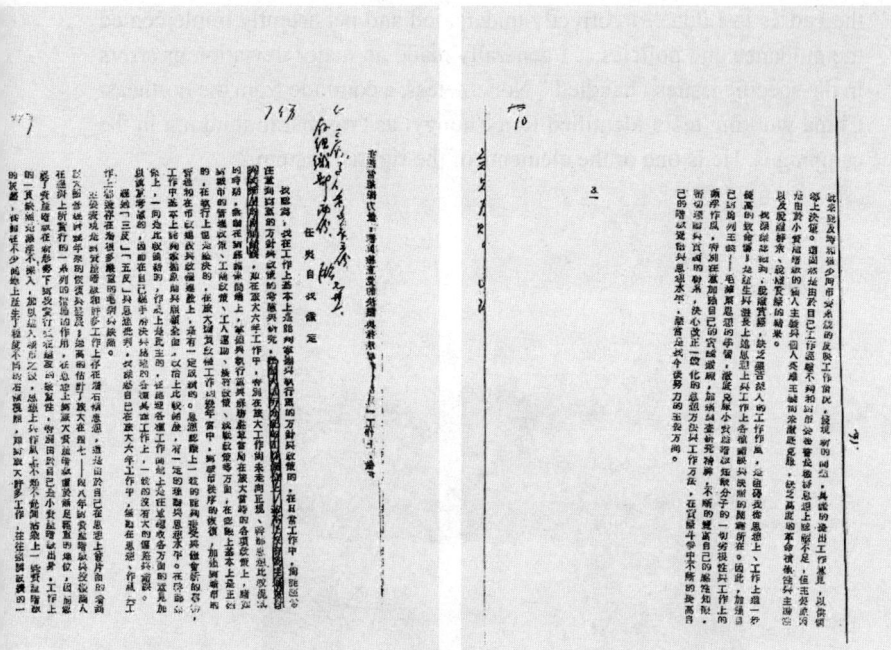

The northeast China bureau working team concluded that Ren Zhongyi was "rightist in thinking in the campaigns"

However, his ideas were strongly opposed by the northeast China bureau working team that took the problems of Lüda seriously and commented that "there are many fat tigers in the high mountains and dense forests" (at that time corrupt officials were called 'little tigers' for embezzling more than Rmb1,000, 'middle tigers' for embezzling more than Rmb5,000 and 'big tigers' for embezzling more than Rmb10,000). They regarded Ren Zhongyi as holding rightist opinions in the political campaigns. In June 1952, the northeast China bureau decided to transfer him from Lüda to work in Songjiang province.

Before leaving Lüda, Ren Zhongyi wrote the following self-analysis: "I think I can basically master and implement the party's guidance and policies and pay attention to the consideration and research of such guidance and policies in my daily work. For instance, in the six years of working in Lüda, especially in the period of chaotic work and thinking of the cadres in Lüda... I correctly understood and persistently implemented the guidance and policies... I generally made no major deviation or errors in the specific issues I handled." Nonetheless, a comrade from the northeast China working team identified Ren Zhongyi as "rightist in thinking in the campaigns. He is one of the elements of the rightist system."

Ren Zhongyi, member of the standing committee and secretary general of Songjiang provincial party committee, on the banks of the Songhua river in June 1952

Before Ren Zhongyi started out to Songjiang province, Ouyang Qin personally came to his home to say a few parting words of encouragement. These words warmed Ren and cemented his determination to strictly implement the party's policies and persist in seeking truth from facts.

Chapter 13

Helping Establish the 'Bright Pearls' of the Republic

On their return from the Soviet Union on 27 February 1950, Chairman Mao Zedong and Premier Zhou Enlai inspected Harbin. "Harbin is the earliest liberated large city in China," Mao said. "Efforts should be made to construct and manage the city, set up more factories, turn Harbin from a consumer city into a manufacturing city and establish it as an example for factories nationwide." Zhou Enlai also required Ren Zhongyi to properly handle factory affairs, professionally train more men, increase output, share experiences and cultivate more cadres.

Ren Zhongyi, second secretary of Harbin party committee, delivers the opening speech at the first session of the first Harbin people's congress in August 1954

In April 1956, Ren Zhongyi was elected as first secretary of Harbin party committee at the first session of the first Harbin congress of party representatives

In July 1953, Ren Zhongyi was elected as second secretary of Harbin party committee. In February 1955, the central committee appointed him to take full responsibility for Harbin party committee. In April 1956, he was elected as first secretary of the committee. As required by the first generation of core leaders of the republic, the Harbin party committee, under his direction, decided to focus on the tasks of 'manufacturing more machines, cultivating more cadres, sharing more experiences and training more skilled workers'.

The vital mission of the first five-year plan of the new China was to centralise all the forces to complete the 156 construction projects that China had designed with the help of the Soviet Union. Thanks to its special strategic position, Harbin undertook 13 of them and became one of the cities undertaking the most key national projects. Ren Zhongyi assumed responsibility for capital construction of the 13 projects and he devoted himself to the task.

Ren Zhongyi (front row, second from left) was elected as a representative of the first national people's congress at Harbin people's congress, August 1954

Ren Zhongyi, first secretary of Harbin party committee, and Lü Qi'en, mayor of Harbin

Ren Zhongyi (second from left) presents a medal to national model worker Su Guangming at the Harbin model worker awards conference

He required supervising leaders to 'give directions at the front line' and that leaders at all levels should spend between a quarter and a third of each month, quarter or year working at the grassroots. He set an example to others by eating, cohabiting, labouring, entertaining and making friends with ordinary workers when he investigated factories and construction sites. He sometimes stayed on construction sites for a series of days, up to as many as 10 days, and was able to solve problems while there. He personally stressed the essential tasks, summarised the experiences of six companies, including Harbin Rolling Stock Plant and Harbin First Tool Factory, inspected and helped identify priorities at 10 plants, and popularised the experiences of a number of model workers of national influence, such as Su Guangming and Wang Sunci. He held enlarged meetings of the standing committee of Harbin party committee in eight key engineering companies and made on-the-spot decisions to promote the progress of work. He proposed the slogan 'door-to-door service' to the municipal authorities. Thanks to his words and deeds, his instructions and appeals were carried out smoothly. According to the requirements of the party committee, there was a citywide upsurge of "contributing necessary and available labour, money, cars and materials and making all efforts for economic and capital construction".

In addition to striving to complete the key national projects, Ren Zhongyi also placed high priority on developing local industries. Harbin used to be a consumer city with strong European influences but extremely backward in light industry and wholly lacking in major industries. He thought that local industries should develop alongside the city's key projects. He held several conferences to study local industrial development and he supported Mayor Lü Qi'en in developing the light chemicals, light textiles, medical and food industries.

Between August and September 1957, the Songhua river in Harbin experienced record floods and Ren Zhongyi (second from right) and Lü Qi'en (far right) observed the dangerous situation and issued instructions in person

During the flood period, Ren Zhongyi (left) and Lü Qi'en held flood-control meetings overnight at home until the following morning, when they would rush to deal with the emergency at the embankments

Harbin flood-control headquarters declared final victory against the city-wide floods on 17 September 1957. Ren Zhongyi (left) and Lü Qi'en, leaders of Harbin, enjoy watching the passing of the peak of this exceptional flood

Ren Zhongyi (back row, sixth from left) and a visiting Romanian party and government administration delegation in front of the landmark flood-control monument in Harbin, October 1964

Ren Zhongyi frequently inspected local industries, giving guidance and directly entering workshops without prior notice. He once inspected a petrochemical plant where the sight of water on the ground dissatisfied him. He lifted up his trouser legs, waded in the water and criticised the factory director. Afterwards, a factory director guilty of a dereliction of duty was removed from office. He once bought a pair of stylish cotton-padded rubber shoes on a business trip and gave them to a rubber plant. Inspired by the secretary of the party committee, the rubber plant was soon producing several kinds of distinctive and stylish cotton-padded rubber shoes. He specially went to Shanghai to investigate the handicraft industry and how it intertwined with people's lives. On returning to Harbin, he talked with leaders of the handicraft industrial development bureau and gave instructions to learn from the experiences of Shanghai and meet people's requirements for 'repair, distribution and patching'.

Ren Zhongyi (front row, third from left) often visited plants to stimulate technical innovation

Ren Zhongyi and a worker study how to improve sock production

Ouyang Qin, first secretary of Heilongjiang provincial party committee (second from left), investigates a plant in Harbin in the company of Ren Zhongyi, member of the standing committee of the provincial party committee and first secretary of Harbin party committee (far left)

Ren Zhongyi often stated that a city could not develop with only 'bones' (large factories) and no 'flesh' (commercial services, or cultural and educational sectors). Harbin experiences long cold winters with relatively few hours of daylight. Darkness and a biting wind dominate the night when workers leave for home. They usually had a quick meal after returning home and then slipped under a quilt on the *kang* (a heatable brick bed). A question came into Ren Zhongyi's mind: since the service sector of the city is so backward and the people live a harsh life, why don't the authorities open the market, invigorate the service sector and encourage poverty-stricken workers, families and citizens to run small-scale snack stands, stores, mills, businesses, land clearing firms and other service industries in their spare time? Won't it help workers and citizens address their everyday difficulties?

Ren Zhongyi with canteen workers

Leaders of Heilongjiang provincial party committee including Ouyang Qin (front row, second from right), Ren Zhongyi (lying in front row, second from left) and Zhang Linchi (front row, far left) inspect coal mines in Hegang. Ren Zhongyi had fainted for lack of oxygen in a roadway and his face turned pale grey

Consequently, while chairing a meeting of the municipal party committee, he decided to promote the 'five smalls' policy and publicly commended workers engaged in developing the service sector. "The municipal authorities encouraged us to run small businesses to supplement the socialist economy, for which we were all moved to tears," said one old man who had been commended. "Although we know we cannot conduct our business on a larger scale, we feel reassured so long as the municipal authorities continue to facilitate and better our lives." However, in the Cultural Revolution, Ren Zhongyi's promotion of 'five smalls' was deemed as a major crime and he was accused of 'staging a return to capitalism'.

Ren Zhongyi headed the municipal party committee and government to complete the first five-year plan one year ahead of schedule in Harbin. The total industrial output value in 1957 increased by 1.14 times compared

Ren Zhongyi accompanies Ouyang Qin and other leaders on a visit to a new type of 'cordwood system' machine tool

with 1952, with an average annual rise of 16.4%. A total of 2,538 new types of product were manufactured from 1954 to 1957, including 30 major sorts of new products that filled gaps in national output and many types of products that ranked first in terms of output nationwide. Forty-three types of products were exported to the Soviet Union, Mongolia, North Korea, Burma, Indonesia, Japan, the UK and elsewhere. In 1949, Harbin's gross output value of industry and agriculture ranked only 11th among 15 major cities nationwide, including Beijing and Shanghai, but it jumped to fifth place in 1957.

Leaders of Heilongjiang and Harbin inspect Harbin Measuring and Cutting Tool Plant. Front row from far right: Li Min, Ren Zhongyi, Tan Yunhe, Ouyang Qin and Chen Lei

Helping Establish the 'Bright Pearls' of the Republic

In July 1964, Kang Shi'en (front row, far left), vice minister of petroleum industry and Ren Zhongyi (front row, second from left) accompany general secretary of the CPC central committee Deng Xiaoping (centre) to visit a rammed-earth house in the Daqing oilfield

Ulan-Fu and Ren Zhongyi accompany Cambodian Prince Penn Nouth to visit the Daqing oilfield in 1972. Front row from right to left: Ulan-Fu, Song Zhenming, Prince Penn Nouth, Princess Penn Nouth and Ren Zhongyi

Harbin began to play a role of supporting national construction as an industrial base. By 1958, it supplied utility boilers, power generators, metallurgical equipment, precision meters and other sorts of tools to more than 20 provinces and cities nationwide. During the first and second five-year plans and the 'three-line construction' periods, major plants in Harbin gave full play to their role as 'incubators', and it also manufactured more equipment, cultivated more skilled workers and produced more materials. A large number of enterprises, such as electric machinery plants, bearing plants, and measuring and cutting tool plants were built in southwest and northwest Harbin, offering vigorous support to the national economy.

The scene outside the venue of the eighth CPC national congress in September 1956, which Ren Zhongyi attended as a representative

Helping Establish the 'Bright Pearls' of the Republic

Ren Zhongyi and Wang Xuan, finance and trade department director of Harbin party committee in Harbin, 1964

Ren Zhongyi, Wang Xuan and their three sons in Harbin, 1965. Back row from left to right: Ren Nianqi, Ren Kening and Ren Kelei

At the eighth CPC national congress in September 1956, Ren Zhongyi made a report to the whole party and the entire nation: "Harbin, one of the cities of key national construction projects, has developed from a consumer city with a weak industrial foundation to a pivotal emerging industrial city based on mechanical engineering." Harbin completed its transformation from a city in need of assistance to one offering assistance and successfully fulfilled the stated tasks assigned by Chairman Mao and Premier Zhou. The three pillar companies − Harbin Electric Machinery Plant, Harbin Boiler Plant and Harbin Turbine Plant − were fondly known as 'the eldest sons of the republic' and 'the bright pearls' by Premier Zhou.

Chapter 14

The First Person to Light up Harbin's Ice Lantern Festival

In late November 1962, Ren Zhongyi headed for a meeting in Guangzhou and, passing through a park, saw a scene of blooming flowers, resplendent coloured lamps and throngs of visitors. He thought to himself: "Guangzhou can hold flower shows and open flower markets thanks to its unique geological and climatic advantages, but Harbin features ice and snow, which means the people are accustomed to staying at home all day long. In a period of national economic hardship, the people lack materials, live a dull spiritual life and seldom go to the park, which remains idle and empty for almost half the year. How can you produce a 'cultural park' in a chilly winter? What should we leaders do to motivate people to participate in outdoor activities and pull themselves together?" It was just before the time of the spring festival of 1963 when Ren returned to Harbin. But he still failed to find a solution to this problem and Harbin people celebrated another dull spring festival by staying at home.

On 1 February 1963, Ren Zhongyi and Mayor Lü Qi'en went to inspect a farm produce fair in Xiangfang district. When Ren Zhongyi left the fair, he noticed a weak light emanating from the door of a roadside household. It came from two hollow chunks of ice made by an old lady squatting at the roadside with buckets, with lighted candles stuck in the middle. The homemade ice lantern was called a 'lamp for the destitute' and in the past was a simple money-saving device for farmers and fishermen along the Songhua river. Some poor families could not afford lanterns on the night of the lantern festival and instead made frozen lampshades at their front gates for fun. However, few people continued to make them any more.

An idea flashed into Ren Zhongyi's mind: isn't the ice lantern a special local product of Harbin? Unlike Guangzhou, Harbin has no winter flowers but it does feature ice and snow rarely seen in Guangzhou. Why don't we produce ice lantern shows in our severe winters?

Warmed by the thought, Ren Zhongyi returned home and asked Wang Xuan, Ren Kening and Ren Kelei to fill buckets and washbasins with tap water and move them to the balcony to freeze. When ice crusts formed, they chiselled the centre of the ice in the room, poured out the unfrozen water in the middle, lighted a candle in the ice crust and made ice lanterns. The family poured black, blue and red ink into the containers full of clean water and froze the water into coloured lanterns. Ren placed the ice lanterns singly or in the shape of a millstone or bottle gourd. He even broke the buckets and washbasins, which were in short supply and rationed in the years of material deprivation.

In early February 1963, the family home served as Ren Zhongyi's workshop to make ice lanterns, which were placed on the balcony. This humble house became the birthplace of China's modern ice lantern festivals

The First Person to Light up Harbin's Ice Lantern Festival

Ren Zhongyi asked Lü Qi'en and Lin Xiaoxia, secretary of the CPC central committee secretariat who lived next door, to come to his home to experiment with the ice lanterns. At nightfall, the courtyards of the three families displayed an extraordinary sight: the crystal ice lanterns on the balconies on the second floor sparkled and could be seen from some distance. That sight brought a smile to the face of Ren Zhongyi, as a plan fermented in his mind.

On 3 February, Ren Zhongyi called together Mayor Lü Qi'en, Deputy Mayor Zhang Ping, Liu Zuotian, deputy director of the municipal construction bureau, and Wang Jun, chairman of the municipal federation of trade unions, to hold a small on-site working conference. He made a bold proposal: "It is 10 January in the Chinese lunar calendar and just five days before the lantern festival. So the spring festival has not ended. Flower shows and flower fairs are held on new year's eve and lantern shows are put on in southern China. We don't have flower fairs or lantern shows. But we can hold an ice lantern show in Zhaolin park on 15 January in the Chinese lunar calendar and call it an ice lantern festival." He elaborated on what he had seen and heard, and invited the participants to view the homemade ice lanterns in the courtyard. He issued the following rallying cry: "We must succeed in holding the ice lantern festival, encourage residents to leave their homes in winter, mobilise the people to make Harbin's winter less of a solitary experience."

Harbin garden engineering office immediately mustered more than 800 workers from 13 departments to make ice lanterns with tap water in Zhaolin park under the direction of Liu Zuotian. Over the next four days, the workers put in long hours, not returning home for supper until nearly midnight. After supper, they allowed themselves just a short nap, and in this short time they created as many as 1,000 ice lanterns. They placed the ice lanterns on mountain slopes, wall supports and branches, installed electric bulbs, candles or embellished the lanterns with tender willow shoots that are a feature of early spring. Harbin Food Company made more than 30 frost flowers from chrysanthemums, live fish and other materials. Students from the arts department of Harbin Art Institute made a sculpture of an elephant out of natural snow. The workers made an ice tunnel and small sledges for children to play with. From Ren Zhongyi's first idea to hold an ice festival, it took just four days and nights to carry it out. What a great achievement! The sheer enthusiasm later became known as the 'ice lantern spirit'.

After Ren Zhongyi made his rallying call to hold an ice lantern festival, more than 800 garden workers made 1,000 ice lanterns in Zhaolin park over four days and nights to ensure the successful launch of Harbin's first ice lantern festival

On the night of 7 February 1963 (14 January in the Chinese lunar calendar), the first Harbin ice lantern festival was opened in Zhaolin park. The ticket price was Rmb0.5 for adults and Rmb0.3 for children. It was a sensation across the whole city, with thousands of citizens enjoying the spectacle. On the first night, almost 50,000 visitors flocked to the park and even the blind were able to 'watch' the ice lanterns with their hands. A few days later, the sheer number of people almost broke the gate to the garden and the park managers had to open it to let them in. The show had been scheduled to run over three days but instead lasted twice as long. In total, 250,000 visitors were received during the six days, accounting for one-tenth of the city's total population. The people, who used to 'stay at home for winter' finally went outside, signalling an end to their former idle lifestyles for six months of the year. Those people who enjoyed the ice lanterns defied severe cold and brimmed with energy.

The day before the opening of the second Harbin ice lantern festival in January 1964. Ren Zhongyi (centre), deputy secretary of the party committee, Guo Weiren (left), and deputy director of the municipal construction bureau, Liu Zuotian, stand on the site of the ice lantern production area

First secretary of the provincial party committee, Ouyang Qin, said: "The ice lantern festival can mobilise people to partake in outdoor activities. What magic power it has!" The Harbin ice lantern festival was the first organised mass event of its kind, ushering in modern ice lantern arts in China and initiating the country's modern ice and snow culture.

From then on, citizens' enthusiasm for the ice lantern festival was insatiable. The second Harbin ice lantern festival opened on 15 January 1964 and it used electric lights, turned natural ice from the Songhua river into ice lanterns, built houses with natural ice, made ice engravings in the shapes of animals, girls and golden foals,[1] and carved elaborate snow sculptures to depict, for example, the god of longevity[2] and children on elephants.[3] Coloured relief ice screens appeared for the first time in the third Harbin ice lantern festival that opened on 1 January 1965. Stage lights and coloured incandescent light bulbs were used in the fourth Harbin ice lantern festival that opened on 27 December 1965, displaying a dynamic, tranquil and gorgeous scene.

A panorama of the ice lantern festival in Zhaolin park, Harbin

An elaborate arch at the ice lantern festival

The families of Ren Zhongyi, Lü Qi'en and Ouyang Qin attend the second Harbin ice lantern festival. Back row from right to left: Liu Zuotian, Ren Zhongyi, Ouyang Qin, Lü Qi'en, Huang Wei (wife of Ouyang Qin), Wang Xuan and Wang Jun (wife of Lü Qi'en)

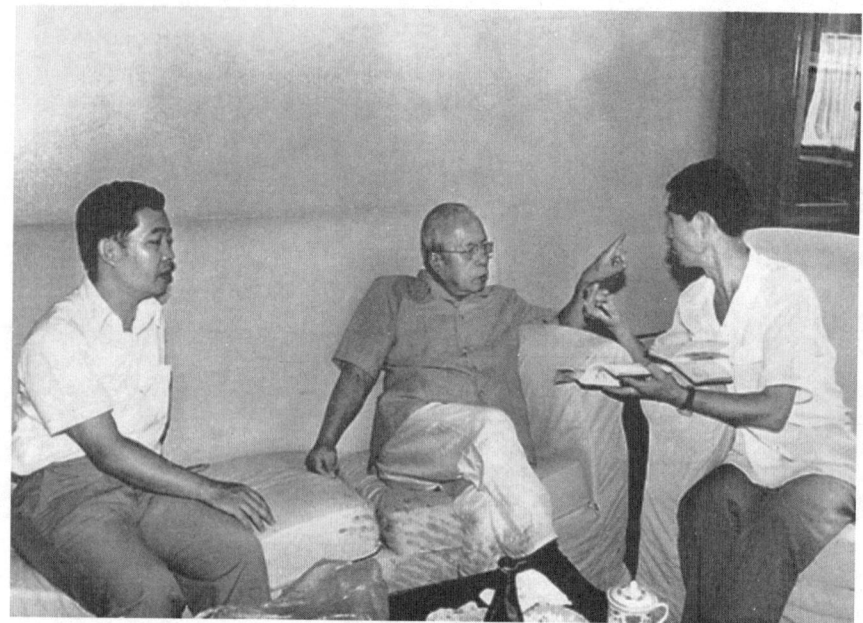

When Ren Zhongyi returned to Harbin in August 1989, ice lantern expert Wang Jingfu (right) seized the opportunity to interview him. Ren disclosed to the media for the first time his original idea for an ice festival and the inside story of how it came about. Pictured left is Ren's secretary Li Ciyan

On 10 February 1963, Wang Xuan, Ren Zhongyi's wife who was then finance and trade department director of Harbin party committee, published *Butterfly Flowers – An Appreciation of Ice Lanterns* under the pseudonym of Huang Xuan in *Harbin Evening News*: "Silvery willows embrace spring and the ice lantern festival, plum blossoms bloom on the Nanling mountains, and the spring comes early in northern China. Frost flowers and sparkles create a beautiful scene and all the people tell the good news to one another. The crystal ice shines in all directions and the light smiles at the stars. Refreshing but not cold, the beautiful heaven takes on a new look." It was the first verse to eulogise the ice lantern in modern China. Afterwards, poet Zou Wenxuan, a member of the standing committee of Heilongjiang provincial party committee and Zou Taofen's younger brother, published four poems entitled *Tour in the Ice Lantern Garden* in *Heilongjiang Daily* in February 1964. The last poem read: "The people of the city paid tribute to Ren Zhongyi, since he brought them a special winter. Southern China boasts cheerful flower fairs and northern China joyously celebrates the spring festival with ice lanterns."

An ice sculpture depicting a dragon playing with a ball at the ice lantern festival

Peacocks spread their tail feathers in the ice lantern garden party

As work on the third ice lantern garden party proceeded at full pace in late 1964, a journalist wrote a report on the event and criticised it as a "waste of resources". For this reason, Heilongjiang Supervision Department dispatched an investigation team. Ren Zhongyi and Lü Qi'en strongly defended the idea. "We chiefly mobilised the workers and young people to build the ice lantern garden party with their voluntary labour," they said. "We spent only a little and did not lose money at all." Ren Zhongyi went on: "It should go ahead even if it did lose money, let alone if it doesn't. This is the orientation of our landscape gardening work." After hearing of the matter, Ouyang Qin said: "Harbin ice lantern festival is good for the economy and for people's physical health. What else could have mobilised two million Harbin people? Harbin ice lantern festivals should be held continuously in future." The investigation team could say little in response, so they left. As a result, the festival continued to be held each year.

An ice tower in the ice lantern festival

The ice lantern garden festival was held only four times before it was interrupted by the Cultural Revolution. It formed a major charge of the criticism and struggle against Ren Zhongyi. Rebels accused the ice lantern festival of 'propagandising feudalism, capitalism and revisionism', the golden foal demonstrating an 'obsession with money' and the god of longevity sculpture of 'preaching the philosophy of survival'. To them, the verse eulogising Ren Zhongyi served to 'glorify the reactionary gang leader Ren Zhongyi'. Zou Wenxuan, the author of the verse, died before being cleared of a false charge in the criticism and struggle.

Thanks to the reform and opening-up initiative, Harbin's ice lanterns were rekindled and the 40th Harbin ice lantern festival was held in 2014. Drawing millions of domestic and foreign tourists every year, it has become the first, longest, largest, most-travelled and most influential ice lantern art exhibition and a dazzling attraction of Harbin and the whole country.

Chapter 15

Amid Chaos, the 'Criticism and Struggle Endurance Champion'

On 16 May 1966, the CPC central committee passed the 'May 16 Notice' and the tempest of the Cultural Revolution suddenly swept across the whole country. Ren Zhongyi, a member of the standing committee of Heilongjiang provincial party committee, permanent secretary of the secretariat of the provincial party committee and first secretary of Harbin party committee, was 'found out' at the start of the Cultural Revolution and became the 'top dog of capitalism in Harbin' and the first secretary

Red Guards in Harbin organise several hundred thousand people to hold a 'meeting to denounce the headquarters', 24 August 1966

of Heilongjiang provincial party committee to be criticised and struggled against in public. On the morning of 26 August 1966, Red Guards searched his house, confiscated his property, locked him in a truck, shouted the slogan "Rebellion is justified" and drove the truck to Baqu stadium in Daowai district, which was renamed Red Guards Square, where a 'meeting to denounce the headquarters' was held.

A fierce sun shone in the sky that day. On the platform, signs were hung around the necks of 'reactionary gang members', including the second secretary of the provincial party committee and provincial governor, Li Fanwu, and secretary of the provincial party committee and vice governor, Wang Yilun. The newly appointed first secretary of the provincial party committee, Pan Fusheng, delivered a speech in which he supported the 'revolutionary activities' of the rebel faction.

A sign reading 'Reactionary gang member Ren Zhongyi' was hung by Red Guards around the neck of Ren Zhongyi, who was criticised and struggled against on the platform, 26 August 1966

Ren Zhongyi stands beside the secretary of the provincial party committee and vice governor, Wang Yilun, during the criticism and struggle session

Red Guards convene in Baqu stadium on 12 September 1966 to criticise the leaders of Heilongjiang provincial party committee and shave the hair of the second secretary of the provincial party committee and provincial governor, Li Fanwu

Amid Chaos, the 'Criticism and Struggle Endurance Champion'

Rebels collectively criticise and struggle against the secretaries of Heilongjiang provincial party committee (Ren Zhongyi is fourth from left), 12 June 1967

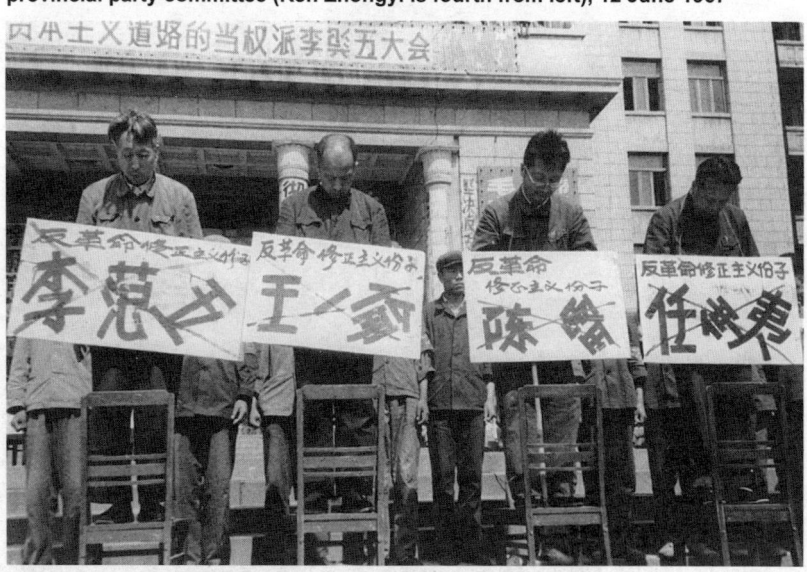

The secretaries of Heilongjiang provincial party committee, including Ren Zhongyi (far right), are collectively criticised and struggled against

Ren Zhongyi: Frontline Fighter and Economic Reformer

Ren Zhongyi sat in the first row of the cement stands. Someone abruptly raised his voice and called out his name purposefully. A leader of the rebel faction immediately grabbed the microphone and shouted himself hoarse: "The presidium of the meeting has decided to criticise and struggle against counterrevolutionary revisionist Ren Zhongyi!" Straight away, the audience responded with the cry: "Down with reactionary gang member Ren Zhongyi."

Ren Zhongyi stood up calmly. Two strong men, sitting either side, pulled him to the platform and prepared a wooden folding chair. It was difficult for Ren to stand steadily on the chair but easy to fall down; any slight move would cause the chair and the person on it to fall. The Red Guards hung a sign reading "Reactionary gang member Ren Zhongyi" around his neck and put a conical paper top hat more than one metre tall on his head. The hat opening was too small to put on, so the Red Guards forced it on with all their strength, causing it to break. A man tied one end of a rope at the back of the top hat and forced Ren Zhongyi to tightly hold the other end with his hands tied behind his back.

Ren Zhongyi is forced to wear a hat and stand on a folding chair with his hands tied behind his back, his body bent double and splashed with ink, 26 August 1966

Someone brought a basin of ink and forced Ren Zhongyi to smear it onto his face with his hands. Later, the person deemed him not black enough, so he held up the basin of ink and exerted his strength to splash it onto Ren Zhongyi, bending his waist at an angle of 90°. In an instant, Ren's face was blackened, with the stinking liquid pouring into his eyes and nostrils and flowing along the tip of his nose and mouth. Then, another man ran onto the platform, taking a writing brush filled with ink and wrote 'Reactionary gang member' on Ren's white shirt. Yet another person held up the basin of the remaining ink, hitched up Ren's collar and poured it down his neck. The ink flowed down Ren's upper body to his waist, legs and feet. The white shirt was splattered with ink and his grey trousers were soaked with ink stains from the inside out. An insane air of excitement permeated all around and brandished fists accompanied the shout "Down with Ren Zhongyi".

When he attended the 15th National Congress of the CPC in the Great Hall of the People in September 1997, Ren Zhongyi met photographer Li Zhensheng. The photo being held by Li, taken 30 years previously, was part of his series *Suffering of the Secretary of Heilongjiang Provincial Party Committee, Ren Zhongyi, in the Criticism and Struggle*. This image won the top news photo award at the '*Arduous Process* National Photography Open Competition'

Li Zhensheng, a photographer at *Heilongjiang Daily* who was on the platform that day, had taken photographs of Ren Zhongyi on many public occasions. Seeing the respected secretary of the provincial party committee insulted in this manner, he felt a rising sense of unspeakable sorrow. He pressed the shutter and recorded the harrowing moment.

Ren Zhongyi could barely stand. His body shook back and forth. Without speaking, he told himself "not to fall down and never let them laugh at me or trample on my dignity! Hold on, hold on and do not lower one's head to the ultra-leftist tide." He was tortured for more than three hours, but he stuck it out.

The sun was burning around noon. The rebels sent him back in a truck. On returning home, Ren Zhongyi knocked on the door gently. Only Wang Xuan and their youngest son, Ren Kelei, who was studying in junior high school, were at home. Kelei was chopping chicken feed in the backyard, and he hurried to open the door when he heard his father's arrival. He was shocked at the sight of his father, before bursting into tears and crying: "Dad…".

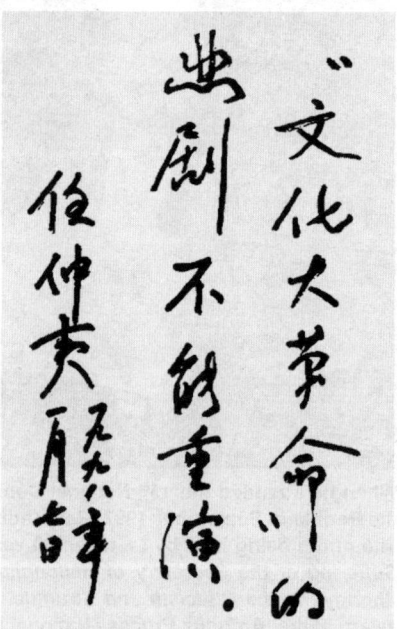

Calligraphy penned by Ren Zhongyi for Li Zhensheng. It reads: "The tragedy of the Cultural Revolution should never be allowed to be repeated. Ren Zhongyi, 7 January 1998"

Ren Zhongyi promptly pointed at the kitchen and said quietly: "Don't tell your mum! I'll have a bath and change my clothes." Not having the heart to disturb his wife, he hurried to wash himself and then came out for lunch. In a calm tone, he said to Wang Xuan: "I'll wear the shirt once it is dyed black." Later, the shirt was dyed black, but the words 'reactionary gang' were still discernible under the sun. But he still wore it all the same and remained unruffled.

After the criticism and struggle, Ren Zhongyi's family were evicted from the dormitory compound of the municipal party committee and moved to a small room in a warren of apartments without a private bathroom. The three family members lived in a small room of just 10 square metres where the furniture, even the chairs, had to be hung on the ceiling or the walls due to the limited space. Since they lived in common residential quarters, the rebels of all units were able to send him, 'Harbin's biggest capitalist roader', to criticism and struggle sessions to show the escalation of their criticism and struggle. For this reason, different groups waited outside Ren Zhongyi's home and competed to knock at his door to send him to criticism and struggle sessions as early as 4-5am every day. Wang Xuan opened the door and reproached them unceremoniously: "Can't you let him live? Is he not allowed to breakfast before he comes with you?" Her stern rebuke quelled the threatening attitude of the rebel faction.

On 12 September, Ren Zhongyi was sent by Red Guards to a criticism and struggle meeting, with his hair 'shaved', a large black sign hung around his neck and his hands tied behind his back. Appearing in this humiliating manner, he was paraded down the street, wearing a top hat that was both taller and heavier than the one in the first criticism and struggle session. He was beaten up and could only stagger through the 'shame parade' that lasted more than an hour. There were many onlookers along the way. A woman model worker could not help crying at the heartbreaking sight but she had to suppress her tears.

Returning home, Ren Zhongyi felt tired both mentally and physically. He asked Kelei to take out the hair clippers and to give him a crew cut for the first time in his life. After that, he lay feebly in bed. At that moment, a postman knocked at the door to deliver a letter. Kelei took it and found it was from Kening, his older brother studying in a college in Beijing. Ren Zhongyi asked him to read the letter for him. It read: "Dear father, I'm sorry to learn in Beijing that you are being criticised and struggled against. No one can better understand you than your sons. We firmly believe you love the CPC and Chairman Mao, and you are definitely not a reactionary gang member or against Chairman Mao. My dear father, I, your son, will always trust you and love you. Wherever you are in future, I will follow you. If you are sent to do farm work, I will do the same with you. Faithful to you always, Kening."

After reading the letter, Kelei heard his father burst out crying, with his face in his hands. He was stupefied because it was the first time in his life that he had seen his strong-minded father cry in this manner. Ren Zhongyi's tears were not shed out of sadness but in disgrace, indignation and struggle, and also for the love, yearning and sense of responsibility for his family. Two minutes later, Ren Zhongyi stopped crying and said in an indignant and resentful manner: "They persecuted and insulted me like that! Had it not been for the sake of your mother and you, I would have put up a desperate fight with them earlier." Kelei knew that the "they" his father mentioned did not refer to the children criticising and struggling against him but the adventurists and schemers behind them, who were attempting to incite people who were unaware of the truth, including the originally innocent children, to blindly 'rebel' and take down a huge number of revolutionary cadres to bring about their evil plot of usurping party leadership and state power.

Ren Zhongyi recollected in later years: "In the first three years of the Cultural Revolution, I attended more than 230 criticism and struggle meetings in front of thousands of people. The largest one was witnessed by hundreds of thousands of people and the small ones were innumerable. All the units I had once worked in would criticise and struggle against me." Each criticism and struggle was noted down in a diary. The rebels discovered it and questioned him: "Are you making restoration records?". He responded straight away: "I did it to learn a good lesson and avoid making such mistakes in future." Actually the 'mistakes' in his mind referred to the havoc that was bringing catastrophe to the party and the state caused by the lawless Cultural Revolution trampling on conscience and justice. According to statistics compiled by Ren Zhongyi, he was criticised and struggled against in more than 2,300 large and small criticism and struggle sessions during the Cultural Revolution. "I became the champion of the most criticism and struggle nationwide," he joked in later years.

Amid Chaos, the 'Criticism and Struggle Endurance Champion'

任仲夷反党反社会主义
的罪恶事实

(内部资料,仅供参考)

毛泽东思想红色造反团原市委机关总团
原哈尔滨市人民委员会红色造反团总团
一九六七年五月六日

Details of the 'anti-party, anti-socialist crimes' of Ren Zhongyi compiled by the rebel faction, 6 May 1967

Chapter 16

Couple Share Good Times and Bad, and Find Liberation in Cadre School

On 20 January 1967, the rebel faction usurped the power of the CPC Harbin party committee. On 16 February, Harbin people's commune was established and it declared "the abolition of all the functions and power of the former municipal party committee and the municipal people's committee and that all power belonged to the commune". The rebels locked up Ren Zhongyi in a 'cowshed', which was a term used exclusively in the Cultural Revolution to refer to a prison set up by rebels for various 'bad characters'. While imprisoned, Ren Zhongyi was allowed to receive visits from relatives and friends. But deprived of any freedom, he endured the hardship of being routinely criticised and struggled against or subjected to reform through labour.

The first spring festival after Ren Zhongyi was imprisoned fell on 9 February 1967. There were no family members around, nor any trace of festivity in the air. In total, he spent four spring festivals and more than 1,000 days and nights in the 'prison'. During this time, he pondered important issues related to the party and the state and was anxious about the fate of the republic. Over countless sleepless nights, he gradually came to the following conclusion: "The Cultural Revolution is by no means a progressive revolution but a historic regression of society. Unless the Cultural Revolution ends, the party and the state will enjoy no peace." However, he firmly believed that the darkness would surely pass and that the party and the people would eventually usher in brighter days.

Couple Share Good Times and Bad, and Find Liberation in Cadre School

Rebels in Harbin smash a sign of Harbin municipal people's committee (municipal government), 16 February 1967

Rebels smash and burn tablets of Harbin municipal party committee and government, claiming they would "abolish all functions and power of the former municipal party committee and the municipal people's committee"

In the autumn of 1970, Ren Zhongyi was released from the cowshed and transferred to work at the 'May Seventh cadre school' on Xinfeng farm in Harbin, together with Lü Qi'en and others. On the farm, he was reunited with his wife Wang Xuan, from whom he had been parted for more than two years. Wang Xuan was labelled as "the greatest capitalist roader of the financial and trade front of Harbin" and she, too, suffered great hardship. The couple had mixed feelings of grief and joy and encouraged each other. He knew from his wife that their youngest son, Ren Kelei, had gone to Changshuihe work farm after graduation from school in October 1968 and he was not able to see him before departing. He also knew that his father in Jinan had died of disease more than one year before. As a filial son, he deplored his inability to have a final meeting with his father.

Rebels in Harbin hold a meeting to declare the establishment of Harbin people's commune in Baqu stadium, 16 February 1967

Although they laboured on the same farm, Ren Zhongyi and Wang Xuan were not allowed to live together. Instead, they lived in separate dorms, although their hearts remained close. Wang Xuan was responsible for cooking and grinding soybeans to make tofu in the canteen. She sometimes took the chance to secretly add one or two steamed buns or ladles of hot soup to her husband's bowl. Ren Zhongyi's task was to do the dirtiest and most tiring farm work, such as driving ox carts and shovelling manure. It was dirty, painstaking and tiring work in the bitter winter. But he always had an optimistic attitude, helped all sorts of 'bad characters' who had been transferred with them, thought about ways to improve the task of shovelling manure and set an example to the other comrades by working hard. Wang Xuan was afraid he would feel the cold and secretly made him a cardigan to wear under his broken cotton-padded jacket, which would be tied at the waist to prevent custodial officers from discovering it and causing trouble.

Ren Zhongyi and Wang Xuan felt even heavier responsibilities on their shoulders after they returned to power in 1971 and 1972. Here, the couple stand on the balcony of their home in Harbin in 1972

In the spring of 1971, Wang Xuan was allowed to leave the May Seventh cadre school and resumed her work as deputy director of the revolutionary committee of Harbin commercial bureau and member of Harbin party committee. In the spring of 1972, she served as deputy director of the revolutionary committee of Harbin (equivalent to deputy mayor) and member of the municipal party committee. After resuming his work in June 1972, Ren Zhongyi acted as a member of the standing committee of Heilongjiang provincial party committee and deputy director of the provincial revolutionary committee (secretary of the provincial party committee after April 1973). He was one of the first leading cadres whose unjust cases were redressed after the downfall of Lin Biao.

Couple Share Good Times and Bad, and Find Liberation in Cadre School

The couple redouble their enthusiasm for work

Ren Zhongyi holds a family meeting

Ren Zhongyi stands in front of a well head in the Daqing oilfield

Couple Share Good Times and Bad, and Find Liberation in Cadre School

Ren Zhongyi braves the severe cold to visit Qiqihar in the early spring of 1974

At that time, Shenyang military region was holding a military production meeting of the three provinces in northeast China in Harbin. On the day of the opening ceremony, the 3,000-seat auditorium was full and more than 120 people were sitting on the platform. The executive chairman of the meeting declared it open and announced the names of members of the presidium. When more than 10 names were declared, Liu Guangtao, deputy political commissar of Shenyang military region, the second secretary of Heilongjiang provincial party committee and first deputy director of the provincial revolutionary committee, who sat in the middle in the front row, got up to speak. "Comrade Ren Zhongyi has been left out," he said. On hearing Ren Zhongyi's name mentioned on the microphone, the auditorium burst into thunderous applause and everyone stood up simultaneously and looked admiringly at Ren Zhongyi on the platform.

When Ren Zhongyi stood up from a corner of the back row on the platform and expressed his sincere thanks to everyone present, another round of applause reverberated around the auditorium, lasting for as long as three minutes. Delegates' hands ached from the clapping and many people's eyes were moist as they welcomed him to resume his work. The prolonged applause did not stop until he was invited to sit beside Liu Guangtao on the front row of the platform.

Ren Zhongyi at a national electronic industry event at Daqing Tongjiang transistor plant on 13 October 1976

Chapter 17

Taking the Lead in the Debate on the Truth Criterion

After the 'Gang of Four' was smashed, the central committee held Ren Zhongyi's performance in Heilongjiang in high regard. On 8 February 1977, they decided to appoint him as first secretary of Liaoning provincial party committee and first deputy director of Liaoning provincial revolutionary committee to arrange for the overall work of Liaoning and turn around the fortunes of the province. To stabilise the situation in Liaoning, the political commissar of Shenyang military region, Zeng Shaoshan, continued to remain as first secretary of the provincial party committee and director of the provincial revolutionary committee.

Ren Zhongyi (centre) and Zeng Shaoshan (right) labouring in Shenyang in 1977

On 7 February 1977, *People's Daily, Red Flag* and *Liberation Army Daily* published the article *Study the Documents and Grasp the Guiding Principles* and highlighted the viewpoints of 'two whatevers': "We should firmly safeguard whatever decisions Chairman Mao has made and we should unswervingly abide by whatever he instructs us to do." The 'two whatevers' became obstacles to setting things right and rectifying the party's 'leftist' mistakes in the Cultural Revolution. On 10 April 1977, Deng Xiaoping wrote to the central committee in his role as a senior CPC member and proposed: "Use correct and complete Mao Zedong Thought to guide the whole party, the whole army and the people of the whole country." In May 1978, a debate on the truth criterion was launched nationwide and the erroneous guideline of 'two whatevers' was resolutely criticised.

Leaders of Liaoning province, including Ren Zhongyi (far left), Zeng Shaoshan (second from left) and the secretary of the provincial party committee and deputy director of the provincial revolutionary committee, Chen Puru (third from left), inspect an underground Yulong coal mine in Fuxin, Liaoning, 1977

People's Daily on 7 February 1977 ran the editorial *Study the Documents and Grasp the Guiding Principles*, expressing its viewpoint on the 'two whatevers'

Without fear, Ren Zhongyi resolutely threw himself into criticising the 'two whatevers'. He thought that, if it was not thoroughly repudiated, the two whatevers would inevitably fester in the minds of millions upon millions of people, keep on dragging the party and the state into the disastrous mistakes of the Cultural Revolution, continue the unredressed injustices for a large number of revolutionary cadres and people who were persecuted in the Cultural Revolution, and reverse the progress of Chinese history.

Back in July 1977, when a publicity work conference was held by the Liaoning provincial party committee, Ren Zhongyi responded to the opinion of "using the correct and complete Mao Zedong Thought to guide the whole party, the whole army and the people of the whole country" proposed by Deng Xiaoping earlier in the same month. He thoroughly analysed the opinion and concluded that he was opposed to the 'two whatevers'. He was the first high-ranking local official to discuss and respond to this opinion. "Practice is one of the most conspicuous characteristics of Marxist dialectical materialism," he stated, and advocated "persisting in the learning style of integrating theory with practice". His opinions were up to one year ahead of public discussion of the truth criterion. It was a pity that this speech was not reported in the press, did not arouse the attention of academics and the press, and brought about only limited influence.

On 11 May 1978, *Guangming Daily* published *Practice is the Sole Criterion for Testing Truth* (hereinafter referred to as *Practice*), which officially raised the curtain on debate about ideology and immediately triggered an argument about 'two whatevers' and seeking truth from facts. The article was rebuked by some central committee leaders.

On 30 June, Ren Zhongyi delivered a speech entitled: *Definitely Persist in the Basic Viewpoint of Seeking Truth from Facts* at the Liaoning provincial party committee petition work conference. "Recently, Vice Chairman Deng specifically talked about the issue of seeking truth from facts at a conference of the whole army on political work," he said. "The theory of seeking truth from facts is the fundamental viewpoint, method and attitude of Marxism and a good style of our party that was always advocated by Chairman Mao. Petition work, like other sorts of work, must persist in this basic view and style. What is the criterion for the solution to the problems of the complainant? Emotional reasoning and subjectivism should be avoided. Truth from facts must be respected... Leaders should not stick to the wrong judgment of a case decided by them or refuse to redress wrong cases for fear of losing face. Nor should they purposefully ignore the rectification of wrong cases originally decided by a certain leader or superior." In the first part of his speech, he stressed persisting in the 'criterion of practice' and, in the second part, he criticised 'two whatevers' and the mistake of refusing to correct mistakes because the "decisions were made by a certain leader".

Ren Zhongyi delivers a speech entitled *Definitely Persist in the Basic Viewpoint of Seeking Truth from Facts* at the Liaoning provincial party committee petition work conference, 30 June 1978

Three days after *Practice* was published, Ren Zhongyi set about writing an article discussing the truth criterion and criticising 'two whatevers'. Finalised in August 1978, the 8,600-word article *Fundamentally Bringing Order Out of Chaos in Theory* was published in the combined eighth and ninth issues of the Liaoning provincial party committee's theoretical journal *Theory and Practice*. In the article, he systematically proposed 'three don'ts' to counter the 'two whatevers': don't be blindly obsessed with 'special identity'; don't consider problems simply from the perspective of class feelings; don't oppose seeking truth from facts because of political expediency. At the same time, he also advocated 'four musts' in the pursuit of seeking truth from facts: first, one must completely and accurately understand and master Mao Zedong Thought, which is the ideological basis of seeking truth from facts; second, one must give full play to democracy and carefully implement democratic centralism, which is the organisational guarantee of seeking truth from facts; third, one must stand by the people and listen to their appeals, which is the way to seek truth from facts; fourth, one must admit that practice is superior to recognition and the sole criterion for testing truth, which is the distinguishing feature of seeking truth from facts.

The article aroused strong reaction in society. *Guangming Daily* reprinted the full text on 9 September.

In September 1978, the central committee decided to appoint Ren Zhongyi as first secretary of Liaoning provincial party committee, director of the provincial revolutionary committee and first political commissar of the provincial military region. Here, Ren stands in the courtyard of Liaoning military region

Taking the Lead in the Debate on the Truth Criterion

On 4 September 1978, Ren Zhongyi was appointed as first secretary of Liaoning provincial party committee, director of the provincial revolutionary committee and first political commissar of the provincial military region. About 10 days later, Deng Xiaoping inspected Liaoning and Ren Zhongyi accompanied him and wrote up the visit on behalf of the provincial party committee. On Deng's special train, Ren presented him with the article *Fundamentally Bringing Order Out of Chaos in Theory*, talked about his viewpoints and received praise from Deng.

Deng Xiaoping, commander of Shenyang military region, flanked by Li Desheng (right) and Ren Zhongyi (left) when Deng inspected Liaoning in September 1978

Ren Zhongyi never ceased fighting. Between September and November, he wrote articles themed on the emancipation of the mind. His 10,000-word article *Emancipation of the Mind is the Great Tide of History* was published in *Red Flag* in December 1978. The article was a continuation and extension of *Fundamentally Bringing Order Out of Chaos in Theory* but with more pragmatism and combativeness. It included yet more condemnation of Lin Biao, the ultra-leftist fallacies of the 'Gang of Four' and the 'two whatevers'.

Deng Xiaoping inspected the three provinces of northeast China in September 1978, where he talked about the problem of seeking truth from facts and said he himself had been "set alight" in north China. Ren Zhongyi accompanied Deng throughout Liaoning, reported work on behalf of the provincial party committee and tacitly understood Deng Xiaoping's thoughts. Here, Ren (second row, far right) accompanies Deng during a meeting with cadres in Liaoning

Taking the Lead in the Debate on the Truth Criterion

In September 1978, Ren Zhongyi presented his article *Fundamentally Bringing Order Out of Chaos in Theory* to Deng Xiaoping on Deng's special train during his inspection tour of Liaoning. Deng praised Ren Zhongyi during this visit. Here, the two men hold discussions outside the train

Ren Zhongyi attends the 11th National People's Congress of the CPC in August 1977 and is elected as a member of the 11th central committee

At the Liaoning provincial party committee publicity work conference in July 1977, Ren Zhongyi responded to Deng Xiaoping's views, made a thorough explanation of 'practicality' and strongly opposed the 'two whatevers'. He was the first high-ranking local official to thoroughly explain his views on these matters

The two official articles of Ren Zhongyi, like sharp knives, cut through to the heart of his criticism on the 'two whatevers'. He mentioned repeatedly that the two articles were drafted by his secretary, Zhang Yueqi, but based on his thinking and accurately expressing his opinions. He regarded Zhang as an outstanding cadre and his right-hand man.

At the two meetings of Liaoning provincial party committee on 20 September and 8 October 1978, Ren Zhongyi systematically expounded the basic principle of Marxism that "practice is the sole criterion for testing truth". He noted that the 'two whatevers' are directly opposed to the 'two whatevers' inherent in seeking truth from facts, namely: "Whatever is proved in practice should be upheld; whatever is proved wrong in practice should be firmly rectified."

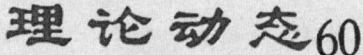

On 10 May 1978, the internal journal *Theoretical Trend* of the party school of the CPC central committee took the lead in publishing *Practice is the Sole Criterion for Testing Truth*

On 11 May, *Guangming Daily* published *Practice is the Sole Criterion for Testing Truth*, which initiated a national debate on ideology

Standing behind Ren Zhongyi and Wang Xuan, from left to right: eldest son Ren Nianqi, second son Ren Kening and second daughter-in-law Chen Xiaomi

At the same time, the first secretary of Gansu provincial party committee, Song Ping and the first secretary of Heilongjiang provincial party committee, Yang Yichen, both aired their support for *Practice*. Ren Zhongyi, Song Ping and Yang Yichen were acknowledged to be among the very first of the provincial party committee first secretaries to participate in the big theoretical debate.

Chapter 18

Refuting 'Two Whatevers' at CPC Central Committee Conference

Ren Zhongyi attended the CPC central committee conference in Beijing from 10 November to 15 December 1978. The conference was preparation for the third plenary session of the 11th central committee of the CPC. At the conference, the participants conducted a fierce discussion on the truth criterion. A brief report of the conference published the article of a certain theoretical authority, which was based on a phone call between this person and the editor-in-chief of *People's Daily*, Hu Jiwei, on the very night when *People's Daily* published *Practice is the Sole Criterion for Testing Truth* (hereinafter referred to as *Practice*).

Ren Zhongyi attends the CPC central committee conference in Beijing from 10 November to 15 December 1978. After meticulous preparation, he made a long speech and systematically refuted the 'two whatevers' viewpoint

The CPC central committee conference in November 1978 made full preparations for breaking the shackles of the 'two whatevers' thinking and for the success of the third plenary session of the 11th central committee of the CPC. Here, central leaders Ye Jianying and Deng Xiaoping meet the participants

The article said that *Practice* was mistaken in terms of direction. It was wrong in theory and denied the relativity of truth and the universal truth of Marxism; it was more seriously wrong politically and intended to tear down the red flag of Mao Zedong Thought, which was unacceptable. The article systematically related 'the whatever faction' viewpoint and was the first official public counterattack of 'the whatever faction' with regard to the discussion on the truth criterion.

After the *Practice* and other articles were published, supporters of the 'two whatevers' could not come up with even a single article to refute them apart from making instructions to prohibit support and pinning labels on political opponents such as "reactionary thought", "mistaken direction", "splitting the party central committee", "targeting Chairman Mao" and "cutting down flags". The decision to publish the 'contents of a phone call' in the brief report of the CPC central committee conference proved to be the parting shot of supporters of 'two whatevers'.

Deng Xiaoping delivers a speech at the third plenary session of the 11th central committee of the CPC

At the crucial moment of this heated debate, Ren Zhongyi came out boldly and made a long speech at the conference. "The article indeed represents the views of some comrades and a trend of thought," he stated. The trend of thought was the 'two whatevers'. He went on: "The essence of the trend of thought is to theoretically draw us to Lin Biao and the Gang of Four and to oppose or prevent our party from making any theoretical or practical progress." He added: "The article of a certain authority pretended to safeguard the great banner of Chairman Mao, distorted and slandered the views of others, and imposed their fabricated wrong ideas onto others."

After that, Ren Zhongyi condemned the four viewpoints of the theoretical authority. In connection with the authority's criticism of *Practice* for "only talking about the standard of practice without mentioning the guiding function of theory", Ren Zhongyi countered: "There is tremendous practical significance to thoroughly discuss that practice is the sole criterion for testing truth. If the problem remained unsolved, it would be impossible to set things right, emancipate thoughts or construct the four modernisations."[1]

The authority criticised *Practice* stating that "advocates doubt everything" and falsely alleged that "since no country in the world has realised communism until now, are Marxist theories on communism really true?" Ren Zhongyi refuted this criticism: "Marxist theory came into being on the basis of solid practice when human society had developed to a certain level. Practice has proved the correctness of its fundamentals. Only the so-called 'authority' and a few followers take it as unproved in practice. On the other hand, many specific concepts and statements of Marxism about communism surely await further testing in future practice and only the authority and his followers deem it unnecessary to further test them through practice."

Responding to the criticism that *Practice* was tantamount to 'cutting down the flag', Ren Zhongyi said: "Practice is the sole criterion for testing truth, which is the fundamental viewpoint of Mao Zedong Thought. Should those who advocate the fundamental viewpoint of Mao Zedong Thought be criticised for 'cutting down the flag' while those who oppose the fundamental viewpoint be praised for 'holding up the flag'? What is the logic?"

Ren Zhongyi votes to pass the resolution of the third plenary session of the 11th central committee of the CPC, which was of great historic significance

Refuting 'Two Whatevers' at CPC Central Committee Conference

People's Daily publishes the *Communiqué of the third plenary session of the 11th central committee of the CPC*

Ren Zhongyi rushed back to Liaoning to transmit the spirit of the third plenary session of the 11th central committee of the CPC. Here, he inspects the implementation of the spirit of the meeting in Ershilipu people's commune in Fu county

Ren Zhongyi (third from right) inspects the implementation of the spirit of the third plenary session of the 11th central committee of the CPC in Anshan and makes Chinese dumplings with the workers there on new year's eve to prepare for the spring festival, 27 January 1979

As to the criticism that *Practice* "blurs the boundary between revisionism and dogmatism", Ren Zhongyi said: "Chairman Mao once said dogmatism aimed to revise Marxism... The Gang of Four opposed Mao Zedong thought by means of direct falsification or not allowing 'the change of a single word'. We should reveal and reject the two methods. To those affected by the thoughts of the Gang of Four, the pernicious influence of the latter method is more serious."

Ren Zhongyi's incisive criticism played a vital role in winning the ideological and theoretical struggle instigated by supporters of the 'two whatevers' at the CPC central committee conference.

In addition to criticising these supporters, Ren Zhongyi also advised the central committee to take a stand on the issue that 'practice is the sole criterion for testing truth' at the conference. "That practice is the sole criterion for testing truth is originally the basic standpoint of Marxism and Mao Zedong thought," he said during a speech on 24 November. "But some departments or conferences of the central committee have passed on a different interpretation... We local officials sense that chaotic thoughts have affected the overall situation and unity." He went on: "If the central committee makes a specific standard and the whole party reaches a consensus, the ideological chaos will be clarified, we will handle local work more easily and the international discussion and speculation about it will surely cease. Besides, those who harbour ulterior motives and attempt to foment dissension and start rumours and slander, will act in vain." Ren Zhongyi's suggestion won the approval of most participants and was largely upheld at the conference. The CPC central committee conference lasted 36 days, much longer than most in the party's history. It paved the way for breaking the shackles of the 'two whatevers' and for the success of the third plenary session of the 11th central committee of the CPC.

Ren Zhongyi (far right) went to Zhaomeng, Liaoning province around the time of the 1979 spring festival to inspect the implementation of the spirit of the third plenary session of the 11th central committee of the CPC. He talks with herdsmen of the Handahan production brigade of Dali commune, Hexigten banner

Ren Zhongyi in Zhaomeng pastureland in the early spring of 1979

The communiqué of the third plenary session of the 11th central committee of the CPC, which was of great historic significance, clearly stated: "The conference praises the discussion of the issue that practice is the sole criterion for testing truth and holds that it boasts far-reaching historic importance for comrades of the whole party and all the people nationwide to emancipate their thoughts and take a correct ideological line. If a party, a country, a people proceed in everything from a bookish attitude and stick to ossified ideology, they will not make any progress; their spontaneity will come to an end and the party and the country will perish."

Ren Zhongyi threw himself into the debate and fully mobilised the cadres and people of Liaoning province to join battle. The Liaoning provincial party committee under his management had officially made decisions and issued notices on 18 August 1978 to launch extensive debate among the people in the province on the truth criterion. In almost one year, the central committee decided to conduct supplementary discussions on the truth criterion among the whole party. It can be said that Liaoning led the debate and became the first province to carry out the most in-depth discussion nationwide. Ren Zhongyi and Liaoning provincial party committee delivered the best performance in the struggle of criticising 'two whatevers'.

Chapter 19

Unswervingly Rehabilitating Wrongfully Accused Zhang Zhixin

In the course of bringing order out of chaos on the ideological and theoretical front, Ren Zhongyi devoted more energy to redressing the many false, unjust and erroneous cases concocted by the 'Gang of Four' and their sworn followers in Liaoning province, and opposed the 'two whatevers' at the organisation level.

On 14 October 1978, Ren Zhongyi condemned the crimes of Lin Biao, the 'Gang of Four' and their trusted and sworn followers at an enlarged meeting of the Liaoning provincial party committee: "They smashed the party organisations and leading organisations at all levels of the northeast bureau, provincial party committee and the grassroots, pinned labels of 'traitors', 'spies' and 'capitalist roaders' on many senior revolutionary cadres and especially the comrades in charge of party committees at all levels... implemented the demarcation of political fronts, defamed a huge number of cadres and people as 'the KMT army'; implemented a fascist dictatorship, fabricated many false, unjust and erroneous cases in the course of purifying class ranks, including more than 1,200 group cases in addition to individual cases implicating more than 100,000 and killing more than 20,000 in the province... drove more than 110,000 cadres and democratic figures in the province to rural areas, including those who were old, weak, ill or disabled and could not escape... All the slander and false charges should be overthrown and all the false, unjust and erroneous cases should be thoroughly redressed."

Thanks to the high priority placed by most leaders of Liaoning provincial party committee, including Ren Zhongyi, on redressing the false, unjust and erroneous cases, the work progressed rapidly in Liaoning. Between May and August 1978, a series of public declarations thoroughly redressed the major unjust cases implicating more than 300 former secretaries of the provincial party committee and former deputy provincial governors, such as the so-called 'KMT-controlled Shenyang spy group case', 'KMT central statistics agency Shenyang spy group case', the 'Shenyang telecommunications office military control intelligence group case' and the so-called 'northeastern gang traitor counterrevolutionary group case'.

By late October 1978, more than 1,300 false, unjust and erroneous group cases involving more than 44,000 people and individual cases involving more than 62,800 people in Liaoning had been assessed. In the whole province, more than 100,000 people were due to be rehabilitated and more than 80,000 had been rehabilitated, accounting for more than 80% of the total who merited rehabilitation. Afterwards, Liaoning provincial party committee redressed the major unjust cases including the 'counterrevolutionary group' case of Liaoyang municipal party committee; rehabilitated the reputation of former leading cadres of the northeast bureau, the provincial party committee and the provincial people's committee who were framed and wrongfully treated in the Cultural Revolution; completely rehabilitated the persecuted; removed the labels from those who were unjustifiably called rightists; and implemented policies for rehabilitated cadres and people. By late 1978, all the major false, unjust and erroneous cases in the province had been redressed.

One of the most notable of the false, unjust and erroneous cases redressed by Ren Zhongyi and Liaoning provincial party committee was the rehabilitation of the wrongfully abused Zhang Zhixin. This was an unjust case that shocked the whole country and caused reverberations at home and abroad.

Zhang Zhixin was born into a patriotic and intellectual family in Tianjin in 1930. She participated in the revolution after liberation, went to college, joined the PLA and the CPC in 1955, and later worked in the office of literature and art of Liaoning provincial party committee publicity department. She had bright eyes, graceful eyebrows, a slender figure, lively character and a love of art. She had been very fond of music since childhood and was especially proficient at guitar and violin. She assiduously studied Marxism and Mao Zedong's works, considered matters deeply and would always ask questions about things she didn't know.

Zhang Zhixin

Zhang Zhixin became a CPC member in 1955

Zhang Zhixin at college. She had bright eyes, graceful eyebrows, a slender figure and lively character

Zhang Zhixin was musically talented and fond of playing the guitar

In the Cultural Revolution, Zhang Zhixin, out of concern for the future destiny of the party and the state, clearly showed her distrust of Lin Biao, doubts about Jiang Qing and dissatisfaction with the practice of overthrowing and framing so many senior revolutionary cadres including Liu Shaoqi, Deng Xiaoping, He Long and Xi Zhongxun. She also frankly criticised the Cultural Revolution and the mistakes of Mao Zedong in his later years. For this reason, she was cruelly persecuted by Lin Biao, the Gang of Four and their sworn followers, and arrested in September 1969. In prison, at court and on the execution ground, she still insisted on truth and remained steadfast and unyielding. On 24 August 1970, she was forcibly accused of being a counterrevolutionary and condemned to life imprisonment. During her long imprisonment, she was severely tortured mentally and physically but she maintained her beliefs and opinions, only to be stigmatised as 'pretending to be insane', 'resisting reformation' and 'stubbornly standing her reactionary ground'. Sworn followers of the Gang of Four declared on 3 April 1975 that she should be put to death. She was executed by firing squad the following day. Before she was shot, the executioners astonishingly cut her throat and brutally killed her secretly for fear that she would yell out the truth. It was a particularly unjust case in the history of modern China.

Zhang Zhixin was especially fond of playing the violin

Zhang Zhixin deep in contemplation during her studies

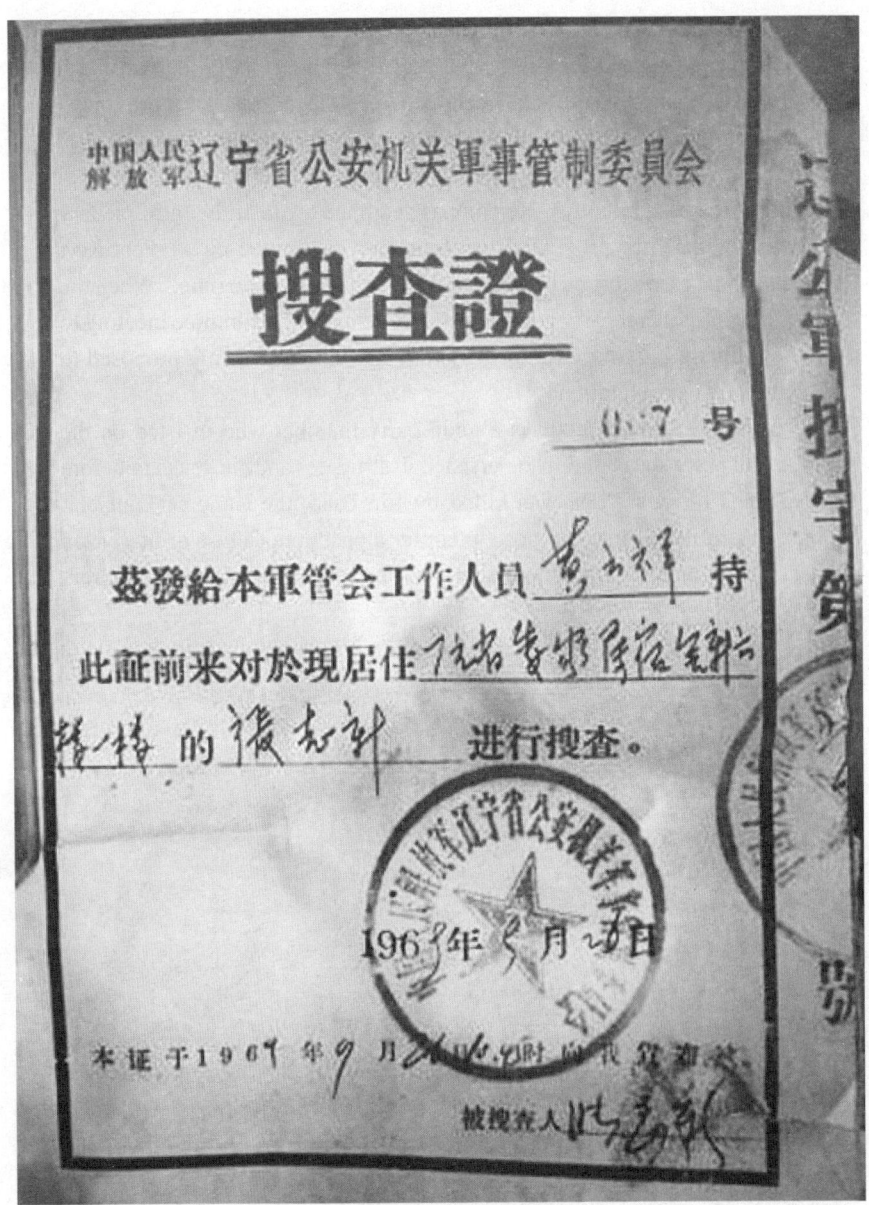

The search warrant for Zhang Zhixin when she was arrested in September 1969

When Ren Zhongyi was transferred to work in Liaoning, Zhang Zhixin had been dead for nearly two years. In January 1979, her wrongful accusation was revealed at an enlarged meeting of Liaoning provincial party committee and it struck a chord with Ren Zhongyi. He stressed at the meeting that "the public security and judicial departments should re-evaluate the case quickly". He emphasised once again at the third plenary session of the fifth provincial revolutionary committee on 11 February: "This unjust case must be re-evaluated and redressed in no time." When the Liaoning provincial party committee held a standing committee meeting to review Zhang Zhixin's case on 9 March, Ren Zhongyi firmly proposed to rehabilitate her reputation.

"Comrade Zhang Zhixin is a good party member who insisted on the truth and party spirit, and who persisted in struggles and chose death before disgrace," he said. "She was killed by Lin Biao, the Gang of Four and their sworn followers. I propose to confer a posthumous title of martyr on her, rehabilitate her reputation, take good care of her family and children,

Zhang Zhixin with her daughter and son

and eliminate the negative influence surrounding this issue. We should hold a memorial meeting in her honour and call on party members and revolutionists to learn from her. The provincial party committee should issue a document in praise of Comrade Zhang Zhixin." He went on: "Comrade Zhang Zhixin was an outstanding Chinese national and had great artistic talent." With Ren's support and backing, a provincial party committee department compiled the *Report on the Review and Rehabilitation of the Case of Zhang Zhixin* within a month. Liaoning provincial party committee made a decision to call on all party members and cadres to learn from the martyr Zhang Zhixin.

Ren Zhongyi took a substantial political risk in firmly redressing the case of Zhang Zhixin and calling on the whole province to learn from her example. At that time, ultra-left thinking was sweeping the country in an attempt to counter the line of the third plenary session of the 11th central committee of the CPC that had taken place not long before. Zhang Zhixin did not simply struggle against Lin Biao and the Gang of Four but also criticised the Cultural Revolution and Chairman Mao Zedong's mistakes, including his misplaced criticism of Peng Dehuai at the Lushan conference. The latter two issues were strictly forbidden topics for discussion in those years. Ren Zhongyi's persistence in rehabilitating Zhang Zhixin indeed required high levels of Marxist theory and policy, pure party spirit, exceptional courage and insight, and decisive boldness. He had to endure pressure from some central leaders. Even the judge who sentenced Zhang Zhixin to death in the original trial claimed to have "convicted her of crimes true to facts" and asked the reviewing judge: "She [Zhang Zhixin] disagreed with Chairman Mao and his works. Can you reverse the verdict for her on the basis of such crimes?" Ren Zhongyi courageously and resolutely bypassed this forbidden topic and set the tone for the rehabilitation on the basis that "Zhang Zhixin was against Lin Biao and the Gang of Four, all her criticism of Chairman Mao was spoken when she was in a confused state of mind, and it was unfair to conclude that she said these words".

At that time, Chairman Hua Guofeng of the CPC central committee happened to visit Liaoning. When he wrote calligraphic inscriptions for some units, Ren Zhongyi suggested: "Chairman Hua, could you please write a tribute dedicated to Zhang Zhixin?" Glancing at Ren, Hua Guofeng ignored him and refused to comply with the request. The cadres beside him noticed the snub, feared that the rehabilitation "would not succeed" and later asked Ren what to do next. Ren Zhongyi responded instantly and with great composure: "He might refuse to inscribe her name for other reasons. It doesn't matter. We will handle it according to the decision of the provincial party committee." This powerful sentence underlined Ren Zhongyi's adherence to party principles no matter what pressure was brought to bear from the paramount leaders.

In the spring of 1979, Hua Guofeng visited Liaoning. When he made inscriptions in Shenyang, Ren Zhongyi asked him to mention Zhang Zhixin but Hua refused. Ren Zhongyi (far left), Zeng Shaoshan (second from left), Li Desheng (third from left) and Hua Guofeng (far right)

Someone later asked him whether he had asked the central committee for permission before he decided to rehabilitate Zhang Zhixin. "No," he answered. "All mistakes should be rectified, which is the obligation of CPC members. There are so many unjust cases that there is no need to ask for approval in the case of Zhang Zhixin." He was clear in his mind that if Zhang Zhixin's case had been reported to the central committee, it would have been almost impossible to reverse the verdict.

On 31 March 1979, the CPC Liaoning provincial party committee held a rehabilitation conference for Zhang Zhixin presided over by Ren Zhongyi. The conference announced the *Decision to Completely Rehabilitate Comrade Zhang Zhixin and Confer on Her the Posthumous Title of Revolutionary Martyr*, and decided to rehabilitate her reputation and party membership and confer on her the posthumous title of revolutionary martyr. On 5 April 1979, *Liaoning Daily* published a long editorial headed *Devoted to the Truth* and publicised for the first time Zhang Zhixin's heroic deeds against Lin Biao and Jiang Qing. Supported by Ren Zhongyi, *Liaoning Daily* publicised Zhang Zhixin's deeds for five consecutive months and published more than 20 special pages of editorial. Ren Zhongyi also advised the newspapers to publish enlarged photos of Zhang Zhixin in prominent positions. After newspapers in Liaoning published the photos, many other newspapers nationwide followed suit. Her graceful beauty and persistence touched many people.

Liaoning provincial party committee holds a conference to rehabilitate Zhang Zhixin, 31 March 1979

The editorial staff of *People's Daily* were extremely touched after reading the long article, decided to reprint it and reported the information to Hu Yaobang, secretary general of the CPC central committee and director of the publicity department of the CPC central committee. "Zhang Zhixin is a heroic figure like Liu Hulan and *People's Daily* should publish her story," said Hu Yaobang. Consequently, *People's Daily* published a long editorial on 25 May 1979 entitled *Struggles for the Truth* to eulogise Zhang Zhixin's heroic deeds. On 11 June, *People's Daily* published an excerpt of her prison diary entitled *Putting the Interests of the Party and the People First* in the editorial.

Li Bin's oil painting CPC Members — Ren Zhongyi, Zhang Zhixin and Hu Yaobang

Xinhua News Agency published a long piece and the *People's Daily* editorial on 25 May and newspapers elsewhere reprinted these articles along with photos of Zhang Zhixin. *Guangming Daily* published Zhang Zhixin's deeds in four pages from 5-13 June, including a long article *A Report Written with Blood* written by a correspondent and memoirs written by Zhang Zhixin's husband and daughter. Articles on Zhang Zhixin also appeared in the 16 June edition of *China Youth News*. It also published the editorial *Learning the Awe-inspiring Righteousness of CPC Members*, which paid a warm tribute to the lofty qualities of Zhang Zhixin.

China was awash with media reports of the awe-inspiring and heroic deeds of the martyr Zhang Zhixin. The sentiments of the Chinese people continued to ferment in the articles, poems and comic strips with the amazing power accumulated for a decade, which soon aroused strong reverberations at home and abroad. Zhang Zhixin's heroic image was deeply engraved in the minds of the Chinese people, vigorously promoted the process of exposing and criticising the Gang of Four nationwide, and stimulated ideological emancipation.

A torrent of articles on Zhang Zhixin appeared in major newspapers nationwide

Instead of being content with rehabilitating and eulogising Zhang Zhixin, Ren Zhongyi went further by suggesting that profound historical lessons could be drawn from her example. He made a speech based on Zhang Zhixin's unjust case at the second session of the fifth NPC in August 1979. Entitled *Drawing the Historical Lessons and Completing the Socialist Legal System – On the Reasons and Related Issues of the Unjust Case of Comrade Zhang Zhixin*, the speech was published in *Workers' Daily* and reprinted in *People's Daily* on 30 August 1979.

Ren Zhongyi proposed to summarise and draw four important lessons from the unjust case of Zhang Zhixin. First, the system of dictatorship should explicitly demarcate crimes from non-crimes in law and political and ideological reaction from criminal offences. Second, the dictatorship over enemies should go through the legal procedure strictly and with legitimate measures. The expansion of the struggles against the enemy and confessions given under duress and inhuman fascist measures adopted in interrogation will inevitably give rise to many false, unjust and erroneous cases among the revolutionaries. Third, socialist democracy and the legal system should be enhanced and the life of the party must be normalised. Fourth, and most fundamental, the plots of schemers such as Lin Biao and the Gang of Four to usurp the leadership of the party and the state must be prevented.

Chapter 20

Not Turning Pale at the Mention of Prosperity and Talking about Becoming Rich

At various meetings in the province between 1977 and 1979, Ren Zhongyi delivered 100 speeches in total, at an average of three a month. The main topic of these speeches was economic construction.

On visiting Liaoning in September 1978, Deng Xiaoping said to Ren Zhongyi: "Efforts should be made to allow some people to be first in creating a better life for themselves." Ren understood that Deng planned to help some people become rich first

When he visited Liaoning in mid-September 1978, Deng Xiaoping said to Ren Zhongyi: "Efforts should be made to allow some people to be first in creating a better life for themselves." Ren Zhongyi had already been thinking the same thing. He understood that Deng Xiaoping planned to help some people become rich first. "His words were simple but of great significance," he recalled. "At that time, many people turned pale at the mention of becoming rich under the influence of ultra-left thinking that equated becoming rich with revisionism. Comrade Xiaoping's words smashed the chains of such thinking." For this reason, wherever he went, he talked about helping people, especially peasants, to become rich and some people to get rich first.

Ren Zhongyi visits Chen Shulan in Xiaochengzi commune, Kangping county, Liaoning, in February 1979. Chen was particularly skilled in raising rabbits but was criticised for doing so. However, Ren praised her: "You set a good example for farmers to develop a sideline and prosper first"

Not Turning Pale at the Mention of Prosperity and Talking about Becoming Rich

In those years, Liaoning's food markets were short of supplies of grain, pork and edible oil. City residents were supplied with 150g of edible oil, 250g of pork and 4kg of tofu each month. Vegetables and other food items were also rationed. The rural situation was even worse and farmers lived a very poor life. When ultra-leftists were wreaking havoc, farmers would be accused of taking the capitalist road for just selling eggs laid by their chickens in the market and bought back some edible oil and salt from the market. They would be forced to 'cease all such capitalist activities'. So farmers would turn pale at the mention of becoming rich.

Ren Zhongyi (third from left) inspects the soil in a field in Jianping county

In February 1979, Ren Zhongyi, Zhao Qi, vice governor in charge of agriculture, secretary Zhang Yueqi and Zhao Fu, editor-in-chief of *Liaoning Daily*, spent more than 15 days visiting five counties in Liaoning: Kaiyuan, Changtu, Xifeng, Kangping and Faku. Wearing a cotton-padded jacket, shoes and hat, Ren Zhongyi looked like an old farmer. He travelled in a jeep, stayed in a guesthouse and ate simple food such as maize stubble, sorghum rice, potato and Chinese cabbage stew, or green beans, spring onion and tofu dipped in sauce. He refused the trappings of power such as official welcoming parties and send-offs. Wherever he went, he not only listened to the leaders' reports, but also went deep among the masses, talked with local cadres, farmers and teachers, and went to farmers' houses to get to know their lives first-hand and hear their aspirations and complaints. He once went to a middle-aged woman's house. Her husband had died long ago, leaving her to bring up three children alone. There was only a broken straw mat on the *kang*. The four family members shared a broken quilt filled with cotton and ate only sorghum, maize and pickles, which failed to fill them up. Ren Zhongyi was saddened at their plight, and said emotionally: "We are terribly sorry for their bitter and poor life so many years after the new China has been founded."

Ren Zhongyi watches ice fishing in Zhaomeng, March 1979

At a third-tier cadre conference in Changtu county on 17 February 1979, Ren Zhongyi delivered his 'three stabilise' speech focusing on the need to stabilise the political situation, stabilise policies and stabilise leadership. He said: "In policy making, don't fear that farmers may become rich, the collective economy of the production team may become rich or some farmers and production teams prosper first thanks to their hard work, good life and greater contributions. Those who become rich first can serve as a model and incentivise others to prosper. That is good, not bad. In the past, the Gang of Four opposed 'prominence' and 'wiped out the rich'. It was totally wrong. Successive prosperity is far better than an egalitarianism that drags us into poverty."

Ren Zhongyi in the countryside

The editor of *Liaoning Daily*, Fan Jingyi, interviews a farmer

On 8 August 1979, the Yingkou municipal party committee held a conference on rural work and focused on the issue of how to make rural life more prosperous. Encouraged by the news, Ren Zhongyi rushed to Yingkou on 9 August and delivered a speech at the meeting on the following day. He began his speech with a startling question: "Why do we come out in revolution? First, we want to 'turn slaves into masters'... The primary purpose of our revolution is to overthrow the 'three big mountains [imperialism, feudalism and bureaucrat-capitalism, which weighed like mountains on the backs of the Chinese people before liberation] and become the master of the country or, according to the lyrics of *The Internationale*, 'to be the masters of the world'... We have triumphantly finished the task of turning slaves into masters. Second, we aim to eradicate poverty and become rich... After becoming masters, we should strive to become prosperous. We have spent three years on adjustment, socialist construction and the four modernisations in a bid to shake off poverty. We work energetically despite all the hardships with the aim of constantly improving people's material, cultural and living standards." "It is a truth and a tenet of socialist development to eradicate poverty and become prosperous. It is the unalterable duty of communists to make our country and people's lives prosperous in socialist construction." "You take a good lead and set a perfect example in the province. All of you present are the forces to organise construction to eliminate poverty and become rich." As soon as he had finished his speech, he received tumultuous applause and the entire audience was warmed to the heart.

Ren Zhongyi (second from right) talks with model workers in Shenyang and praises them for their contributions to prospering the country and the people

After receiving Ren Zhongyi's draft speech on 29 August, editorial staff at *Liaoning Daily*, including Fan Jingyi, felt embarrassed. Normally, a speech by the first secretary of the provincial party committee would be published unaltered. However, it included the phrase "the purpose of revolution is to get rid of poverty and become rich", which sounded quite original and direct after many years of being told that people should 'turn pale at the mention of becoming rich'. "The objective of revolution is surely to annihilate the bourgeoisie," said the editors in discussion. "How can becoming rich eradicate poverty?" After 'prudent consideration', the editors finally decided to take the following precautionary measures: first, the article should not appear on the front page; second, the headline font size should not be large and it should exclude the term 'purpose of revolution'; third, the name of the correspondent should be omitted in case of possible retribution.

On 30 August, *Liaoning Daily* published an article entitled *At the Rural Work Conference of the CPC Yingkou Party Committee, Comrade Ren Zhongyi Advocates the Four Modernisations and the Efforts to Become Rich*, which was buried on an inside page. In early September, *People's Daily* published an abstract of Ren Zhongyi's speech. On 2 September, Liaoning provincial party committee endorsed the Yingkou party committee's *Report on How to Accelerate the Prosperity of Yingkou*. Yingkou immediately launched a discussion on how to accelerate rural prosperity and became the first city in the province to pursue the goal of rural prosperity.

Ren Zhongyi (second from right) and Chen Puru (far right) accompanied by Li Xiannian, vice chairman of the CPC central committee and vice premier of the state council (third from right) and Chen Yonggui, vice premier of the state council (fourth from right), study initiatives to increase agricultural production, 1978

In contrast to *Liaoning Daily*, which published the article on efforts to achieve prosperity, many other provinces and cities took a more cautious approach. For example, a daily city paper asked the municipal party committee for instructions: "Liaoning is publicising how to become rich, shall we follow its example?" The municipal party committee rejected the idea: "No. Liaoning did it, but we should not. We should not mention the idea without instructions from our superiors."

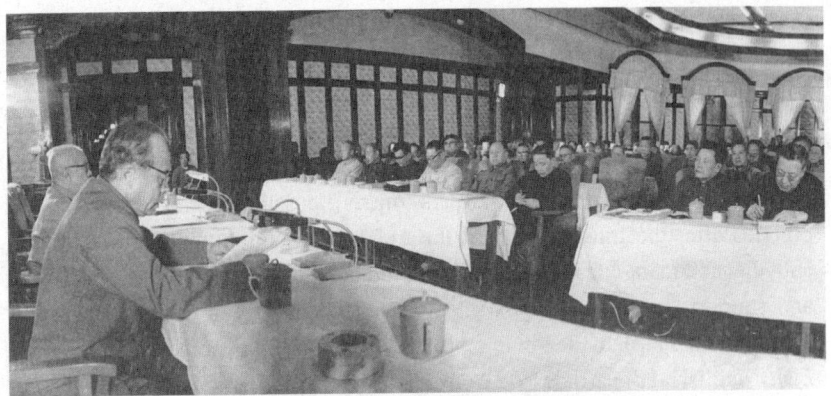

At the CPC Liaoning county party committee conference in November 1979, Ren Zhongyi calls on the whole province to hold a discussion on "the courage, possibility, methods and support of achieving prosperity"

Ren Zhongyi (third from right) visits the cultural centre in Kezezuo county, Liaoning, August 1979

At the CPC Liaoning county party committee conference on 17 November 1979, Ren Zhongyi, on behalf of the provincial party committee, called on the whole province to hold discussions on "the courage, possibility, methods and support of achieving prosperity" and encouraged farmers to "eradicate poverty and become rich". In his long speech, Ren systematically looked at the inevitability, feasibility and urgency of becoming rich in the context of the objective of revolution, the essence of socialism and the living conditions of farmers. He also made a comprehensive narration on the courage (eliminating the pernicious influence of 'turning pale at the mention of becoming rich' in farmers' minds), possibility (the favourable policies after the third session of the 11th central committee of the CPC and the abundant local resources), methods (the ways to become rich) and support (leaders and departments at all levels should offer vigorous support and help) of achieving prosperity. On 21 November, *Liaoning Daily* published the article *The Courage, Possibility, Methods and Support of Achieving Prosperity* with a splash headline on its front cover.

The call of Ren Zhongyi to achieve prosperity was instantly embraced by all people in the province. Although one person threatened to report him to the central committee, he did not flinch but instead encouraged people to work harder to achieve prosperity. An epoch-making discussion on rural prosperity was held in Liaoning, including Shenyang. The discussion shattered the restrictions that had previously tied rural cadres and people; broke through the forbidden guiding principle of class conflict and established the concept of focusing on production; smashed the forbidden notion that 'distribution according to work is the foundation of capitalism', implemented economic policies in rural areas and mobilised the enthusiasm of rural cadres and people; countered the idea that 'becoming rich is revisionist' and allowed a few communes and commune members to become rich first; broke through the forbidden zone of 'grain production as the guiding principle' and 'transition in poverty to a higher stage', conducted affairs according to the laws of economics, and further emancipated and developed productivity. The discussion on achieving prosperity fired up the entire province and everyone competed hard to be among the first to become rich. Various inventions of the people won the zealous support of Ren Zhongyi and the provincial party committee. Leading authorities at all levels also initiated innovative activities to facilitate wealth acquisition in the local area. Liaoning's economic development had taken on a more promising outlook.

Not Turning Pale at the Mention of Prosperity and Talking about Becoming Rich

Ren Zhongyi and Li Desheng visit a rural area in Liaoning and delight in the bumper harvest

Ren Zhongyi tries in vain to persuade Hua Guofeng to build Dalian into a special economic zone in north China, Dalian, late June 1980

At a cadre meeting in Yingkou county in August 1979, Ren Zhongyi asked: "What's your per capita annual income?" A loud voice responded: "Rmb200." That year, the average per capita annual income in Yingkou was Rmb118, the 'highest level' in the whole province. It was regarded as quite exceptional for an individual to earn Rmb200. But Ren Zhongyi said: "A total of Rmb200? So little! You should strive to earn Rmb500 in three years." After hearing his words, the meeting place fell silent, but was soon followed by a burst of laughter. "Why do you laugh?" asked Ren. "Your laughter is surely not because you are happy or confident. You were shocked by the figure of Rmb500! You were scared and burst out laughing, disbelieving what I said. Actually, as long as you emancipate your mind, make every effort, develop production and explore new possibilities for prosperity, you can surely achieve the goal of earning Rmb500 per capita in three years time." Hearing what the first secretary of the provincial party committee said, the cadres no longer dared to laugh, but they still thought the ambition was unrealistic. "Is it possible to multiply income two point five times in just three years?"

Later, Ren Zhongyi recounted this exchange to Fan Jingyi, who said: "When the per capita annual income in the rural area of Yingkou county reaches Rmb500, I will surely write an article that mentions this episode." Three years later, Fan went to Yingkou county and was told that the average income of Rmb500 had indeed been achieved. He deeply admired the foresight, courage, resolution and sagacity of Ren Zhongyi and fulfilled his promise to publish the story in his newspaper. The article was entitled *In a Place Where Someone Was Scared to Laugh*. By then, Ren Zhongyi had been transferred to work in Guangdong province. When Fan Jingyi mailed the article to him, Ren replied with great joy.

Chapter 21

Received by Nine Central Leaders Before Governing Guangdong

In late October 1980, General Secretary Hu Yaobang said to Ren Zhongyi: "You previously urged the building of an SEZ in Dalian, but it was impossible. However the central committee has decided to appoint you to govern Guangdong where SEZs have been established." Ren Zhongyi replied with the following suggestion: "Can one of the present first or second in command in Guangdong, Xi Zhongxun or Yang Shangkun, still take the lead in Guangdong while I work as second in command?" Hu Yaobang responded: "They have already been appointed to other posts. Just go ahead."

Soon afterwards, Xi Zhongxun made a phone call from Guangdong to the Shenyang authorities, urging Ren Zhongyi to take up office in the southern province. By that time, Xi Zhongxun and Yang Shangkun had been given free rein by the Guangdong central committee to implement special policies and flexible measures and establish the SEZs in Guangdong. They had also made significant progress in carrying out work for the reform and opening up of Guangdong. Since the central committee transferred them to assume more important tasks in Beijing, the heavy duty to take the lead in launching reform and opening up fell on the shoulders of Ren Zhongyi.

The first secretary of Heilongjiang provincial party committee, Yang Yichen, said to him with sincerity: "Comrade Zhongyi, you'll either win great honour in Guangdong or commit a major crime." Ren Zhongyi knew what his comrade-in-arms meant: being a pioneer of reform and opening up in the SEZs would involve venturing into many forbidden zones and minefields and taking huge political risks. He was then 66 years old. He had performed well in Heilongjiang and Liaoning, was held in high regard by the party and the people, and achieved both success and fame. It was not flowers but thorns that awaited him in Guangdong. However, given the backing of the central committee, the call of the great cause of national reform and the ardent expectations of the Guangdong people, Ren Zhongyi marched ahead resolutely and without hesitation.

The first secretary of Heilongjiang provincial party committee, Yang Yichen, told Ren: "Comrade Zhongyi, you will either win great honour or commit a major crime in Guangdong"

On 9 November 1980, the CPC central committee officially appointed Ren Zhongyi as first secretary of Guangdong provincial party committee. The department director of light industry, Liang Lingguang, was made secretary of Guangdong provincial party committee and first secretary of Guangzhou municipal party committee. From 31 October to 6 November, before taking up their posts, they were each received by nine central leaders – Ye Jianying, Deng Xiaoping, Li Xiannian, Hu Yaobang, Zhao Ziyang, Wan Li, Wei Guoqing, Yao Yilin and Gu Mu, who gave them their encouragement, support and direction. It was rare for the central committee to attach such importance to the appointment of two provincial-level cadres. It was a reflection of the central committee's commitment to Guangdong and the pilot reform and opening-up process.

The vice chairman of the central committee, Ye Jianying, told them: "Guangdong is a good place, with a developed education, favourable water transport and numerous overseas Chinese who are enthusiastic to help build the motherland. Oil has been exploited in the Pearl river estuary. The people living in Guangdong's mountainous areas live on what the land can provide them and decide to develop the mountainous area." Commander-in-chief Ye Jianying held their hands tightly and urged them again and again to pay attention to unity. "Efforts should be made to properly handle the relationship between external and local cadres," he said.

Ren Zhongyi understood what Ye Jianying meant. He was from Hebei and Liang Lingguang was from Fujian. Neither of them was closely connected to Guangdong or even knew Cantonese. In the 1950s, two 'anti-localism' campaigns were fabricated in Guangdong. More than 30,000 local cadres were implicated or punished. The mental and physical trauma experienced by cadres would take more than two decades to resolve. The campaigns had devastating consequences at home and abroad and were the source of the most serious unjust cases in Guangdong.

Ren Zhongyi in Zhongnanhai before taking up office in Guangdong

The vice chairman of the central committee, Ye Jianying, greets Ren Zhongyi

"Please rest assured," they said, repeatedly. "We are able to get along with people from all corners of the country and properly handle the unity between external and local cadres." Ye Jianying looked at them trustingly and smiled: "I'm relieved."

Later, they paid a visit to the vice chairman of the central committee, Deng Xiaoping, who said to them: "The SEZs do not merely refer to places such as Shenzhen and Zhuhai. It's by no means enough to simply develop these areas; you should give full play to the advantages. You need to formulate laws and come up with good ways of running SEZs." They responded: "The central committee requires us to develop Guangdong to be a pioneer and pacesetter for the whole country, and open up new opportunities with creativity and a pioneering spirit. We will do our utmost to meet the requirements of the central committee."

Comrade Xiaoping stressed the importance of making good use of the policies. Referring to the sound changes introduced in Liaoning thanks to the favourable policies in recent years, he said: "There's a big difference between doing well and poorly. Good policies will give rise to obvious improvements once implemented. The work of administering Guangdong should also start with making the best of policies and mobilising enthusiasm."

Mentioning the historical problems of Guangdong, Comrade Xiaoping said: "The situation in Guangdong is extremely complicated. We should not dwell on the past, which is difficult to disentangle. Let bygones be bygones. Of course, it wouldn't do to completely forget the historical problems. Such problems should be handled comprehensively. All parties in previous conflicts should be considerate about the other party's position rather than get tangled in historical opposition. It's the only way forward. We should encourage people to look ahead."

Finishing their official business, they chatted about art. Ren Zhongyi talked about his view of a naked painting that was on display in Beijing's airport terminal. He said to Comrade Xiaoping that modern artistic works adopted stereotyped writing and the people had made jingles to satirise the stereotyped stories: "The production team leader makes mistakes. The branch secretary comes to help and asks farmers to air their grievances. They end up catching a spy." Comrade Xiaoping burst out laughing. "Your viewpoint is right," he said.

They talked with Comrade Xiaoping for an hour and a half. After they left, they reflected on what Comrade Xiaoping had said and agreed to handle the historical problems of Guangdong according to the principle of 'extensive' rather than 'intensive' handling as required by the central committee.

On another occasion, they met Comrade Hu Yaobang. Ebullient and having a creatively agile mind, Hu Yaobang replied while constantly gesturing: "Guangdong boasts ideal conditions and has great potential." "There is a ballad that goes: 'No sea is better than the North Sea / no province is better than Lianzhou.' I wrote my own version: 'No province is better than Lianzhou, where the mountains, waters, forests and fields are all treasures / If the fourth five-year plan is implemented properly, the per capita income of Rmb1,000 will surely come about.' That is to say, it is very possible for us to achieve an average per capita national income of Rmb1,000." He then changed the topic of conversation: "You should highlight the present difficulties and key issues in Guangdong. There are problems concerning energy, transportation and agriculture ahead of us. But the most fundamental problem is ideological discord." He added: "Everyone has their own bitter experience of the past. Let bygones be bygones. We should assess the performance of cadres with regard to the future, especially your performance and your working style. All cadres, external or local, old or new, are good cadres as long as they accomplish great achievements in their work. It won't do for cadres to work inattentively or slowly, as if they were doing tai chi. Much better to work as if taking part in Shaolin boxing." He also said meaningfully: "Chairman Mao once talked about a couplet in the temple of a high official in Chengdu relating to how to govern the inland province. Now I quote it to you: 'If psychological attack is feasible, the wicked will retreat without fighting because they realise their inferior strength and submit willingly, without daring to plot another rebellion; it is wrong to take lenient measures or strict and impartial steps without sizing up the situation. Governing Sichuan requires thorough consideration.' Now, I change a word from the second line of the couplet for you: 'It is wrong to take lenient measures or strict and impartial steps without sizing up the situation. Governing Guangdong requires thorough consideration.'"

Ren Zhongyi and Hu Yaobang talk cordially

Received by Nine Central Leaders Before Governing Guangdong

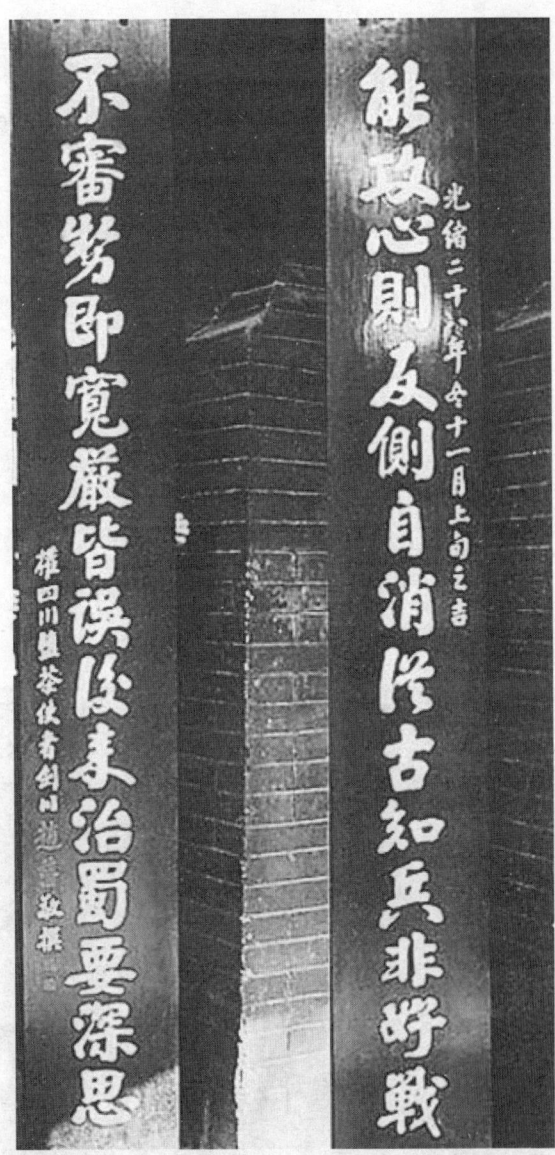

Hu Yaobang presented Ren Zhongyi and Liang Lingguang with a couplet from the temple of a high official in Chengdu, relating to how to govern Sichuan, which Hu altered to apply to Guangdong. The picture shows the couplet in the temple

Ren Zhongyi very much liked the couplet given by Hu Yaobang. Here at home, in his later years, he reproduces the couplet with a calligraphy brush

Vice premier of the state council, Wan Li, visits Guangdong and talks cordially with Ren Zhongyi

Received by Nine Central Leaders Before Governing Guangdong

On 8 November 1980, Ren Zhongyi took a flight to take up duties in Guangdong and was given a gracious welcome by Xi Zhongxun. The two secretaries, old and new, cordially shake hands with each other

Ren Zhongyi (left) and Liang Lingguang in the office of Guangdong provincial party committee on 11 November 1980

Ren Zhongyi had a keen sense of the significance of the changed word. He understood that the first line of the couplet summed up the importance of winning popular support and the second line conveyed the view that policies must start from reality, take into consideration the current and specific situation, and adapt to the changing circumstances in order to implement good governance of Guangdong.

They also came to the office of vice premier Wan Li. "You should emancipate your minds and have a free hand to invigorate the economy and blaze a new trail," said Wan Li. "It doesn't matter if you make some mistakes. The state council will be responsible. Even if you do make mistakes, it is of great significance to the whole country for you to take the first step and offer some lessons for others to learn from. You should invigorate the economy in Guangdong and refuse to implement departmental regulations if they are unsuitable for Guangdong." He added: "The stress should be on economic development and improving people's lives in a stable, accurate and rapid manner. Focusing on economic development that bears fruit is always the right way."

On 11 November 1980, Ren Zhongyi (far right), Liang Lingguang and Xi Zhongxun (centre, front) and Yang Shangkun (far left) were among those who went to inspect Guangzhou

Guangdong provincial party committee hold a conference on 18 November 1980 to announce the appointment of Ren Zhongyi (standing) as first secretary of Guangdong provincial party committee. Front row, second from right: Xi Zhongxun; front row, far right: Yang Shangkun

Accepting these orders, Ren Zhongyi and Liang Lingguang took a flight on 8 November to take up their duties in Guangdong.

On 18 November, the CPC Guangdong provincial party committee held a party member and cadre conference above city and provincial levels in the Guangzhou Sun Yat-sen Memorial Hall. When Xi Zhongxun announced the central committee's notice to appoint Ren Zhongyi as first secretary of the CPC Guangdong provincial party committee, up to 5,000 cadres burst into thunderous applause to show their welcome for the new secretary who was famous for ideological emancipation, moral integrity and extraordinary intelligence and determination.

Ren Zhongyi stood up and nodded greetings to everyone present. First, he outlined the main contents of the discussions he and Liang Lingguang had held with the central leaders and then gave his views on the future work in Guangdong. He concentrated on Deng Xiaoping's instruction to "start with the work in Guangdong from implementing the favourable policies" and Hu Yaobang's suggestion to "win popular support" and "size up the situation". Instead of talking about Guangdong's various difficulties and problems, he intended to look forward and aim high, focusing on the implementation of the central committee policy that the province should take the first step. "Special policies should be implemented really specially and flexible measures should be adopted really flexibly," he said. "Guangdong should really take the first step. Otherwise, it will all be empty talk." As a result, the 'three reallys' became the first slogan attributed to Ren Zhongyi after he assumed office in Guangdong. The cadres in the hall felt their spirits and strength rise. Thunderous applause broke out once again.

The guideline of 'three reallys' proposed by Ren Zhongyi later won the approval of Deng Xiaoping and of the central committee secretariat, and it stood as the objective of the struggle of cadres and ordinary people in Guangdong.

After taking up office, and in partnership with Governor Liu Tianfu, Ren Zhongyi broke through the obstacles to redress the case of anti-localism in Guangdong. Based on the work of his predecessors, Xi Zhongxun and Yang Shangkun, he presided over the standing committee meeting of Guangdong provincial party committee and decided to submit to the CPC central committee in April 1982 a report to remove the wrong wording of 'imperative' to criticise and struggle against Gu Dacun and Feng Baiju and of the 'imperative' to fight against 'localism', and to eliminate the bad practice of 'localism'. With the support of central leaders such as Hu Yaobang, Huang Kecheng and Xi Zhongxun, and conquering mountains of obstacles, the CPC central committee finally issued a notice in February 1983 to thoroughly rehabilitate Feng Baiju and Gu Dacun. Ren Zhongyi managed to lift the inhibitions of numerous cadres in Guangdong province, won their showering praise and support, enabled them to throw themselves into opening up the new situation of 'three reallys' and laid vital foundations for the leading personnel for fresh progress in Guangdong.

Chapter 22

Proposing 'Three Let Go More' in National Economic Adjustment

In December 1980, a couple of months after Ren Zhongyi arrived in Guangdong, the central committee held a meeting to discuss national economic adjustment.

The meeting advocated a policy of economic adjustment necessitating drastic cutbacks on the capital construction front and adequate retrenchment elsewhere. Many construction projects across the country

Deng Xiaoping at the central committee meeting

were either shelved or suspended. All ministries and commissions of the central committee issued orders stating that Guangdong and Fujian were no exception. The Ministry of Finance changed Guangdong's fiscal responsibility system and ordered the province to turn over more than 85% of the surplus. It was beyond what Guangdong could bear.

Deng Xiaoping made it clear at the meeting that certain things should be maintained. "The decision to set up several SEZs in Guangdong and Fujian should continue," he pledged. "However, the steps and methods should comply with the adjustment and progress at a slower tempo."

Ren Zhongyi (far right) and Liang Lingguang (front left) visited the SEZs in the same month they took office. Here, they are pictured in Zhuhai SEZ

In accordance with the strategic proposal, Ren Zhongyi assessed the situation and made daring changes according to Guangdong's special circumstances. He delivered four speeches at the central work conferences from 17-22 December. "I applaud the decision of the central committee to adjust and stabilise the economy," he said. "The Guangdong government has decided that all construction projects that don't conform with the regulations of the central committee should be stopped; some enterprises should suspend operation; the five small business types and enterprises run by communes and production brigades should be reorganised;

administrative intervention must be implemented and enhanced where necessary." But he stressed: "The fundamental objective of centralised and unified intervention aims to invigorate the economy and improve industrial and agricultural production and the national economy as a whole." He repeatedly cited Chen Yun's opinions in speeches made in the 1950s and 1960s that "stress should be placed on overall balance and centralised and unified intervention as well as economic invigoration but not in a uniformly rigid manner." "Comrade Chen Yun once talked about the issue, saying we should continue to implement whatever conforms to the present realities without any hesitation."

Ren Zhongyi and some provincial and city leaders in Zhuhai SEZ on 25 November 1980. From right to left: Wu Nansheng, Wu Jianmin, Ren Zhongyi, Fan Xixian, Liang Lingguang and Guan Xiangsheng

He solemnly expressed his opinion: "I hope the central committee and the state council can stress not only centralised and unified administrative intervention but also economic invigoration and the integration of the two so that cadres and the masses do not mistakenly view this as a policy change. A policy U-turn is 'troublesome', which will trigger fluctuations and losses and should be avoided. Our experience in socialist construction over three decades proves that it is difficult to invigorate the economy but quite easy to bring it to deadlock. The economy has been a little bit invigorated over recent years thanks to great efforts but may slip back if we are negligent. Some departmental cadres are accustomed to rigidly unified intervention and it is fairly easy for them to fall back if any change arises."

He proposed that such one-sidedness should be prevented in the following three ways:

First, draw a clear demarcation. Centralisation and invigoration should be continued where necessary. "In the past, there was a saying: 'Invigoration leads to disorder, disorder leads to unification and unification leads to death'. Why? The answer lies in the measures used to handle the disorder. We should analyse a specific problem or policy rather than cancel reform simply due to the existence of this problem."

In January 1981, Ren Zhongyi took on the additional role of first political commissar of Guangdong military region

Second, the power to make decisions and handle affairs should be delegated to lower levels. Administrative intervention should avoid too many meticulous and rigid restrictions and interventions. The central committee granted Guangdong government great power and issued a document stating: "The central committee authorises Guangdong government to take flexible measures, implement suitable instructions and requirements of the central departments and to refuse to implement, or implement flexibly, those that are unsuitable." It seemed that the central authorities were reneging on their promise to Guangdong that it could operate with this degree of freedom.

Third, policies should be relatively stable and consistent. "It seems a little more money can be made if these policies are declared to be cancelled," he said. "But, as a matter of fact, there is no increase in production, no accumulation of extra social wealth and, instead, there is a sapping of confidence among cadres and the masses in the policies. This sets back enthusiasm and destroys productivity in the long run."

Ren Zhongyi visits Shantou sensitive photographic chemical plant, 25 March 1981

He went on: "The documents of the central committee and the state council all say that the central committee is determined to implement special policies in the two provinces and that this guideline will not change." "Comrade Xiaoping said: 'The so-called SEZs do not just refer to some specific areas but to all of Guangdong and Fujian. It does not refer to economic invigoration in those small areas but to Guangdong and Fujian as a whole. That is to say, special policies should be implemented across the two provinces'." He continued with a heavy heart: "We are most concerned whether the special policies can be carried out in Guangdong. Unexpectedly, our concerns have materialised early on in the reform process. If the good policies were to be cancelled, the so-called special policies for Guangdong would fizzle out and the policies made by the central committee would be overthrown." He earnestly requested: "The central committee should not frequently change its policies. We hope the central committee and the relevant departments of the state council will support and safeguard the policy of the central committee."

After returning to Guangdong, Ren Zhongyi implemented well-considered policies on adjustment and organically integrated reform, development and adjustment for better development. He proposed the guiding principle of 'three unifys' at a CPC Guangdong provincial party committee conference on 16 January 1981: to unify the adjustment and implementation of special policies, to unify 'centralisation' and 'invigoration' and to unify 'drastic curtailment' and 'advancement'. He stressed that implementing adjustment did not mean cancelling the special policies and flexible measures but, on the contrary, to perfectly combine the two. He further emphasised that centralisation and unification should be carried out where necessary; invigoration should also be continued where necessary rather than held back. Economic invigoration must help to eliminate difficulties, make adjustments, and achieve an improvement in productivity and people's satisfaction in a flexible fashion. Ren Zhongyi also laid stress on progress despite consistent but radical cutbacks, fostering strengths and circumventing weaknesses through adjustment and developing Guangdong's economy in a more stable, healthier and more dynamic way in a bid to enhance development in the long term.

Proposing 'Three Let Go More' in National Economic Adjustment

After the central work conference, Ren Zhongyi returned to Guangdong and proposed the well-considered guideline of 'three unifys' in January 1981

At the Guangdong provincial party committee meeting on 15 May 1981, Ren Zhongyi said adjustment did not mean an end to reform but simply a slowing down of reform; if other places in China slowed down by two steps, Guangdong could slow down by one step. Guangdong should be allowed to grow faster than other places because the central committee required it to take the first step

At the Guangdong provincial party committee meeting on 15 May 1981, Ren Zhongyi said: "Adjustment does not mean an end to reform but instead we should focus on combining adjustment with reform. The central committee allows us to adopt special policies and flexible measures to launch reform. If other places in China slow down by two steps, Guangdong can slow down by only one step. Guangdong should be allowed to grow faster than other places because the central committee requires it to take the first step."

At a work conference of the state council on the SEZs in Guangdong and Fujian from May to June 1981, Ren Zhongyi introduced the 'three let go more' initiative for overall work in Guangdong. First, the province should be more open to the outside world, including making positive

At a work conference on Guangdong and Fujian in May 1981, Ren Zhongyi introduced the 'three let go more' initiative, which involved being more open to the outside world, adopting more flexible internal policies and delegating more power to lower levels. This initiative served as the guiding principle of the two provinces to implement special policies and establish the SEZs

use of overseas Chinese capital and foreign capital, introducing suitable, advanced technology and scientific management methods, and expanding foreign trade to prosper the three SEZs. Second, it should adopt more flexible internal policies, including implementing internal reform of the economic system, allowing various economic elements to coexist, properly handling the relationship between a planned economy and market regulation, attaching more priority to the role of the market economy by better utilising the laws of value and other economic levers to invigorate the economy. Third, more power should be delegated to lower levels, including expanding the power of the two provinces in areas such as the economy, human resources and local legislative power; the provincial government should delegate power to subordinate governments, expand the autonomous rights of enterprises and delegate many rights that enable enterprises to make specific economic decisions.

Ren Zhongyi visits Pingshi town, Lechang county, in northern Guangdong mountainous region, 1981. From right to left: Yang Yingbin, Zhang Yueqi and Ren Zhongyi

The central committee approved Ren Zhongyi's proposal of the 'three let go more' initiative on 19 July, which served as a guiding principle of the two provinces in implementing the special policies and establishing the SEZs.

Under the lead of Ren Zhongyi, the provincial party committee adopted effective policies, overcame many difficulties, suspended the operation of up to 1,000 small-sized steelmaking and chemical engineering enterprises that were inefficient in terms of production or energy consumption, laid emphasis on developing light industry as well as food, electronics, household appliance and textile businesses, and set up a light industrial structure with 'Guangdong characteristics'. Zhujiang Water (a soft drinks company), Guangdong Grain (a manufacturer of food, including biscuits), and electronic products and household appliances that were made in Guangdong quickly won a nationwide reputation. In the adjustment, the economy of Guangdong and the SEZs did not fall back but increased at high speed, demonstrating that the province really was 'taking the first step'

Ren Zhongyi at the Guangzhou Nanhu hotel to pay an advanced new year's visit to Ye Jianying on 4 February 1981

in the country. The cadres and people of Guangdong began to appreciate Ren Zhongyi's ability to navigate through a complicated situation — closely integrating the policies of the central committee with the local realities, underpinned by the principle of stability combined with strategic flexibility. They were filled with heartfelt admiration for the courage and insight of Ren Zhongyi.

Chapter 23

Cracking Down on Smuggling and Twice Ordered to Beijing

On 11 January 1982, the CPC central committee issued an emergency notice to the whole country instructing a strict crackdown on those cadres in Guangdong's coastal regions engaged in smuggling, illegal peddling, profiteering, embezzlement and bribe-taking. The notice was reported in a briefing from the commission for discipline inspection of the CPC central committee. At that time in some of Guangdong's coastal

Guangdong coastguards crack down on coastal smuggling, 1981

regions, there were fishermen who did not catch fish, workers who did not work, farmers who did not farm and students who did not study, but instead touted for smuggled goods like a swarm of bees along roads and in streets and lanes. The smuggled goods included contraband radios, electronic watches, television sets, clothes and socks from Hong Kong. With the introduction of foreign capital, embezzlement, bribe-taking and abuse of power for personal gain were on the rise in Guangdong.

During talks about smuggling in Guangdong in January 1982, Vice Premier Gu Mu warned: "Comrade Zhongyi, Guangdong is a subject of heated debate now"

In quick response to the emergency notice of the central committee, Ren Zhongyi held various meetings requiring the whole province to firmly crack down on economic crimes. The Guangdong provincial party committee set up a special leading group to investigate such cases. The leaders of the commission for discipline inspection of the CPC central committee also headed a team to investigate cases in Guangdong. Vice Premier Gu Mu warned Ren Zhongyi: "Comrade Zhongyi, Guangdong is a subject of heated debate now."

From 11 to 13 February, the secretariat of the central committee held a conference on the work of Guangdong and Fujian and instructed 18 party and government leaders of Guangdong, headed by Ren Zhongyi, to travel to Beijing. This was a rare event in the history of Guangdong. At the conference, Ren Zhongyi, provincial governor Liu Tianfu and others reported on the extent of smuggling, illegal peddling, embezzlement and bribe-taking in Guangdong and outlined the measures taken by the provincial party committee strictly in accordance with the facts. However, the leaders of Guangdong did not report to the central committee in time, so the central committee was not kept abreast of the latest situation and the briefing of the commission for discipline inspection of the CPC central committee reflected cases months before. In the previous year, Guangdong held two major, province-wide anti-smuggling campaigns and restricted large-scale smuggling and illegal peddling operations. With several departments deploying a joint crackdown, smuggling and illegal peddling were now on the decline rather than on the rise. Ren and Liu also reported accurately the achievements since the implementation of the special policies and flexible measures in the hope that the central committee would not reverse the special policies granted to Guangdong.

Nonetheless, a sour atmosphere pervaded the meeting room. Someone said Guangdong had lost control of smuggling and illegal peddling; others claimed the province would collapse within three months if things continued in the same fashion; there were calls for tough measures and the killing of some leaders 'as a warning to others'. Since a declaration had been made that no political campaigns would be waged after the Cultural Revolution, the punishment of Guangdong's leaders should be called 'a nominal campaign'. Since smuggling was not a capital offence, some proposed a modification of the criminal law. It was unusual that copies of *The Origin of the Concessions in Old China* compiled by the research department of the central committee secretariat were handed out at the conference. Someone said the nature of Guangdong had changed. The lost ground should be retaken, unlike in the past when concessions were given to foreigners. All this meant that the conference was not merely an attempt to solve economic crimes such as smuggling and illegal peddling, but also a discussion of whether the SEZs should be continued or expanded in future.

At the conference, Xiang Nan whispered to Ren Zhongyi: "After two days, it has only just occurred to me that originally it was Fujian that was 'implicated', but in fact it's you."

In the face of censure and suspicion, Ren Zhongyi still proposed to introduce clear legal distinctions when it came to handling smuggling: to separate errors made at the workplace due to insufficient experience from illegal criminal activity; to separate smuggling, illegal peddling and profiteering from the correct implementation of special policies and flexible measures; and to separate individual corruption from non-individual corruption. Those cadres who commit general economic errors should be criticised and given strict education and receive reduced or suspended punishment. But some people in charge of the central committee disagreed and thought the treatment was too lenient. They advocated severe punishment as a warning to others. Ren Zhongyi stood his ground: "Some grassroots cadres made errors at work due to the policies and regulations of the province and the provincial party committee and government should take the blame." Later, the central committee agreed with his view and wrote it into the minutes of the meeting, which gave protection to a large number of cadres.

The central leaders, including Hu Yaobang, explicitly said the central committee would not change the policies for Guangdong but that they should summarise the experiences and move ahead. Guangdong was required to implement the emergency notice of the central committee more firmly and effectively, further correct their ideology and better implement the special policies and flexible measures.

A couple of days after the conference, Hu Yaobang made a call to Ren Zhongyi, instructing him to return to Beijing because the members of the standing committee of the political bureau were still confused and in need of reassurance because some problems had not been 'worked out'. Ren Zhongyi was well aware that it was Hu Yaobang himself who needed reassurance. Consequently, he asked that he travel to Beijing with Liu Tianfu because he had only recently started work in Guangdong and was less familiar with the situation. So Ren Zhongyi and Liu Tianfu left for Beijing again, which was later called 'the second report in Beijing' by the people of Guangdong.

On 19 February, the leaders including Hu Yaobang convened a meeting with Ren Zhongyi, Liu Tianfu and the first secretary of Fujian, Xiang Nan. They passed on the instruction of the standing committee of the political bureau, rigorously criticised Guangdong for the ineffective implementation of the spirit of the central committee and required Guangdong to pay close attention to the struggle against bourgeois liberalisation in the economic

Ren Zhongyi was recalled to Zhongnanhai in February 1982. He endured huge pressure and had a heavy heart in the face of criticism and censure

field. A view prevailed at the conference that Guangdong's reform impacted the planned economy and that its work was not "lacking in invigoration" but "much too invigorated". It was also expressed that Guangdong "had become inured to the unusual and had become accustomed to it". Some even asked, provocatively, whether Ren Zhongyi was a CPC member, adding that it was easy for capitalism to develop in a place like Guangdong. They deemed it necessary for Guangdong to be administered by hardliners rather than those who had a quick wit.

After the meeting, Ren Zhongyi felt a mix of emotions and was heavy in heart. He thought: Guangdong's reform has just made its first step and scored some initial success only to encounter a 'campaign'. It will be difficult for Guangdong to continue due to the effect of the campaign. Some said Guangdong had been "much too invigorated". But, in truth, there is still much scope to invigorate those relatively under-developed parts of Guangdong needing invigoration. The task of invigorating the economy is never complete; more can always be done. Otherwise, it is not

Deng Xiaoping greets Ren Zhongyi and You Taizhong, commander of Guangzhou military region (left), during the spring festival of 1982 at a gathering of soldiers and civilians in Guangzhou

invigoration. Some said Guangdong "had become inured to the unusual and accustomed to it". Actually, it was their own limited experiences that had caused the surprise. They could not accept the arrival of new leaders and new initiatives. So they blamed without scruple and exerted too much intervention. They asked whether I was a CPC member, while fully knowing that I am. Am I not a CPC member as a secretary of the CPC provincial party committee? This criticism was a reflection of the dissenting opinions of the central leaders in the area of reform and opening up.

Just two weeks earlier, Comrade Xiaoping came to Guangzhou to enjoy the spring festival. At that time, the central committee had issued the emergency notice. He told Ren Zhongyi: "The policies decided by the central committee are correct and you can continue with the reform if you think it is good." Ren Zhongyi thought he, as a CPC member, should unswervingly implement the guideline and policies of the central committee and Deng Xiaoping's instructions. He would never waver on the issue of reform and opening up and the establishment of the SEZs.

One evening, a film was shown in the auditorium of Zhongnanhai. Ren Zhongyi asked his son, Ren Kelei, who was working in China's import and export commission, to watch it with him. Soon after the film started, Ren Zhongyi walked from the front row to the back row and said to Ren Kelei: "The film is not interesting. Let's have a walk outside." They arrived at the lakefront, where a thin layer of ice had settled on the lake surface in the chilly spring air. A cold wind made them uncomfortable. "Recently, some central leaders expressed dissatisfaction with the work in Guangdong and I may be transferred," Ren Zhongyi said in a low voice. "You should be psychologically prepared for it."

As it turned out, Ren Kelei already had a hunch that this might happen. Ten days earlier, he had sent files to Jiang Zemin, deputy director of the import and export commission. Jiang, who directly participated in making the decision to set up the SEZs and had always supported reform and opening up and the establishment of SEZs in Guangdong, asked him to sit down. "Your father has recently been working under huge pressure," he said. "The higher authorities have expressed dissent about Guangdong." Ren Kelei answered: "Yes, it is always difficult to satisfy both the higher authorities and local requirements." But when he heard his father's words, he still felt an unbearable chill in his heart.

Ren Zhongyi and his secretary Zhang Yueqi often recalled the event in later years. The next day Hu Yaobang asked Ren Zhongyi to have a separate talk, so Ren and Zhang Yueqi went to him. "The superior authorities think your implementation has been inadequate," Hu Yaobang said "Would you make a self-criticism to the CPC political bureau?" Ren Zhongyi responded: "We've carefully implemented the guideline and policies of the central committee. What is the self-criticism for?" Hu Yaobang asked with concern: "Comrade Zhongyi, did you ever say that you advocate profiteering?" After pausing to think, Ren Zhongyi replied: "When I talked about the import and export of cane sugar at the Guangdong foreign economic relations work conference, I said: 'We often make a loss if we export cane sugar when the international price for sugar has dropped due to bumper harvest, and import sugar when the price rises due to poor harvest. We should do the reverse: aim to import when prices are low and export when they are high. Profiteering is not allowed at home but we should learn to 'profiteer' in foreign trade and make more foreign currency'. It was said in jest." "I see," said Hu Yaobang after bursting into laughter. "In short, you should rethink the matter profoundly and write a self-criticism," he continued, "Ziyang and I have already made our own self-criticism!"

Ren Zhongyi and provincial governor Liu Tianfu talk about how to solve the problems in Guangdong in 1982

General secretary of the CPC, Hu Yaobang, asked Ren Zhongyi to write a self-criticism to the CPC political bureau

Returning from the meeting, Ren spoke of his way of thinking and Zhang Yueqi transcribed his words. They drafted a self-criticism that very night. The contents included: how they started the reform and opening-up process; paying too much attention to the task of how to better introduce foreign capital and projects but too little to the problems that might arise as a result of reform and opening up; discovering and solving the problems after they appeared and being slow to react.

That next morning, once Liu Tianfu's ideas had been solicited, the self-criticism was sent to Hu Yaobang. After carefully reading it twice, Hu approved the self-criticism and put it away. After Ren Zhongyi handed in the self-criticism, the members of the standing committee of the central committee, including Deng Xiaoping and Hu Yaobang, decided not to punish him. So he could finally escape the torment.

The self-criticism was written by Zhang Yueqi and no office copy was kept on record. Later, Ren Zhongyi once said that it was his only self-criticism to the central committee and he hoped to find a copy of it. But his wish remained unfulfilled until his death.

Chapter 24

'Three Unswervinglys' Policy Sustains Guangdong Reform and Opening Up

Ren Zhongyi bore huge pressure from all sides. The central committee and various departments took back the import and export rights granted to Guangdong. Some inland provinces and cities withheld and froze many commodities that had been smuggled from Guangdong. Sales people from Guangdong were shunned in business activities in other provinces and cities, and some were treated as smugglers. Either their certificates were confiscated or they were detained without reason. Some provinces and cities even made explicit instructions prohibiting their sales staff from doing business in Guangdong. Guangdong was turned from a bustling province to a desolate market. Ren Zhongyi was persuaded in private: "Can we still talk about reform and opening up? No newspaper in Beijing has recently published any articles on the subject." Ren Zhongyi replied: "But the central committee does not prohibit us from talking about it."

The difficulty Ren Zhongyi faced was how to transmit and implement the spirit of the central work conference on the two provinces to the whole province. If the guidelines issued at the conference were transmitted completely, the enthusiasm of cadres and the masses of Guangdong for reform and opening up would be inevitably dampened. Explicit instructions were given at the conference to investigate and punish a group of cadres. But Ren still firmly believed that a large majority of cadres in Guangdong were innocent. Some central leaders suggested debating the problems to reach a common understanding. Ren thought it unwise because debate would lead to deviation or even political campaigns like those in the past that were raised to a higher plane of principle and two-line struggle, where people were accused arbitrarily and had labels pinned on them unjustly.

Before returning to Guangdong, Ren Zhongyi said to Hu Yaobang: "There is not a communiqué of the conference. There are some sections or phrases that are not suitable to be communicated in part or in whole. For instance, 'This is another savage onslaught on us by the bourgeoisie' and 'We would rather suffer losses in business in order to carry out the struggle to the end'. The slogan 'Never forget class struggle' written in big characters during the Cultural Revolution near Zhuhai wharf has still not been erased, and it can be seen clearly in Macau. If this slogan were repeated, it would trigger misgivings in Hong Kong, Macau and abroad and raise suspicions among mainland Chinese that our policies have been changed."

The gate of the Guangzhou Zhudao hotel. From 20 March to 3 April 1982, Guangdong provincial party committee held a provincial three-level cadre conference to communicate and implement the spirit of the central committee conference on the two provinces

Hu Yaobang did not mince his words: "You yourself can decide what is said." On balance, Ren Zhongyi decided to apply the carte blanche advocated by Hu Yaobang and not to convey anything unfavourable for the reform and opening up of Guangdong and the implementation of the special policies or anything that might arouse ideological chaos inside and outside the party.

After returning to Guangzhou, Ren Zhongyi and Liu Tianfu passed on the instructions of the standing committee of the central committee to the standing committee of the provincial party committee. They held a standing committee meeting lasting four-and-a-half days for them to clarify their personal problems and conduct criticism and self-criticism. On 26 February, the information was delivered to cadres above the rank of provincial bureaus and those in charge of prefectures, cities and counties.

The lotus pond pavilion of the Guangzhou Zhudao hotel is located in front of the site of the provincial three-level cadre conference to communicate and implement the spirit of the central committee at the conference on the two provinces. Before the conference, no one was in the mood to appreciate the elegant scenery outside and a sense of panic pervaded everyone

A provincial, prefectural (municipal) and county-level conference was convened over 15 consecutive days from 20 March to 3 April. Before the conference, many people expected a fierce atmosphere and several county party secretaries were prepared for self-criticism, criticism and struggle as well as investigation. Some had even brought their luggage, fearing they may be detained. Everyone was in a state of panic.

On 1 April, Ren Zhongyi gave a summative speech at the provincial three-level cadre conference in the auditorium of the Guangzhou Zhudao hotel. His opening remarks were delivered amid a grave atmosphere: "This meeting is not about condemnation but encouragement." These remarks brought utter silence to the auditorium.

In his speech lasting more than one hour, he covered the following issues: the importance of, and reason for, soberly and correctly recognising economic crimes and avoiding attributing rampant economic crimes to the policy of reform and opening up; cracking down on economic crimes strictly according to the policies without making a major fuss, forcing everyone to pass a test or launching a mass movement; rigorously rectifying the economic chaos, continuing with strict management based on the realities and insisting on the orientation of economic invigoration; correctly treating foreign businessmen and never regarding them as being corrupt or bad because most overseas Chinese and Hong Kong and Macau compatriots love their country and hometown, abide by Chinese laws and conduct business in the proper manner.

Ren Zhongyi mentioned three other interesting aspects.

First, the decision of the central committee that Guangdong should take the first step was correct. We should soberly recognise the gravity of economic crimes as well as the achievements of implementing the special policies and flexible measures. Without clearly recognising the former and imposing a severe crackdown, the reform and opening up would not advance soundly; without clearly recognising the latter, we would be seized with panic and lose forward impetus. The former was the tributary and the latter was the trunkline. It would be wrong to mistake the tributary for the trunkline.

Second, the 'two unswervinglys' policy was proposed – unswervingly cracking down on economic crimes and unswervingly implementing reform and opening up and internal economic invigoration. After the conference, Ren also proposed to "unswervingly implement the policy of bringing prosperity to people's lives". Together, they were known as the 'three unswervinglys' policy. He reiterated the 'three let go more' initiative – 'to be more open to the outside world, to adopt more flexible internal policies and to delegate more power to lower levels'. To avoid the vicious circle of 'treatment leading to chaos and control leading to death', he changed the previous guideline of 'opening to the outside world, invigorating the domestic economy, applying more management to invigoration and achieving greater invigoration with more management' to 'opening to the outside world, invigorating the domestic economy, looking ahead ideologically, strengthening management, applying more management to invigoration and achieving greater invigoration with more management'.

When Ren Zhongyi walked into the auditorium of the central building of the Zhudao hotel and began to deliver a summative speech, he wore a confident smile rather than a solemn look

Third, responsibility should be taken in order to protect a great number of cadres. "The cadres and masses of Guangdong have been working diligently, making arduous effort and contributing to national construction and changing the appearance of Guangdong," he said with sincerity. "The faults chiefly lie with the provincial party committee." "Among those in the provincial party committee, I should take primary responsibility for these problems." "I should not be exempted from responsibility for problems that existed or were decided before I took office."

After the provincial three-level cadre conference ended, Ren Zhongyi (third from left) went to visit the seaside in Haifeng county and drew up a plan to crack down on smuggling

Before concluding his speech, he encouraged them emotionally: "The provincial party committee requires leaders at all levels to brace themselves and strive harder. The provincial party committee and government will be responsible for their past wrong decisions and instructions, while those who implemented these orders are not to blame. You are still allowed to make mistakes and correct such mistakes in work so long as you do not violate the law and rules or commit crimes. Cadres who are filled with untiring energy and a pioneering spirit should be encouraged. Those who achieve brilliant things at work deserve praise from the party organisation. It is totally wrong to take a passive attitude or to be afraid of difficulties. Every cadre should make a positive effort, work audaciously and endeavour to achieve more."

The earnestness of Ren Zhongyi deeply moved all participants, who gave him sustained applause and many tears were shed in excitement. A county party secretary felt a whirl of emotions: "I'd thought it would be a ferocious conference. Instead, it turned out to be impassioned."

Ren Zhongyi (second row, fifth from left) with local cadres on Hongchang square in Haifeng county. Ren encouraged them to carry forward the glorious traditions of the Haifeng people, including the martyr Peng Pai, and achieve more in reform and opening up as well as construction

Ren Zhongyi wrote an open letter to the purchasing agents across Guangdong, affirmed their hugely important role in developing the commodity economy, admitted they were impacted by being shunned in their business dealings with other provinces and the state, and asked them to brave the difficulties and do their work well. The letter warmed the hearts of the purchasing agents like a spring breeze. With their eyes filled with tears, they spread the news excitedly. They knew the provincial party committee understood and supported them and they would live up to the high expectations of the provincial leaders.

Ren Zhongyi delivers a motivational speech at the provincial 'strict crackdown' mobilisation conference on 15 August 1983

Zhang Yun (back row, third from left), vice chair and deputy secretary of the leading party group of the All-China Women's Federation, and cadres of the federation in the early 1960s

The slogan 'three unswervinglys' proposed by Ren Zhongyi and his strength of personality to assume responsibility calmed the nerves of the cadres and the masses and made them firmly believe that the policies of the party had not changed, which significantly protected and mobilised their enthusiasm to implement the policies of reform and opening up so that Guangdong registered remarkable achievements in cracking down on economic crimes and invigorating the economy. That event won profound praise from cadres and the masses in Guangdong and was talked about approvingly for more than 30 years. A group of cadres at that time said: "But for Ren Zhongyi's persistent support for the reform and opening up under pressure, Guangdong would surely have taken on another look and would not be like what it is today."

Ren Zhongyi (far right) visits Zhelang commune in Haifeng county to investigate serious smuggling and illegal peddling in May 1982

In December that year, Zhang Yun, a member of the advisory committee of the CPC central committee and a former deputy secretary of the commission for discipline inspection of the CPC central committee, conducted a two-week special research project on Guangdong, wrote an investigation report to the central committee and essentially affirmed the work done by Guangdong province generally and by Ren Zhongyi individually. Deng Xiaoping immediately wrote instructions to circulate the report among members of the standing committee of the political bureau. Ren Zhongyi took this as support by Deng Xiaoping for the work of Guangdong and himself. After that, he felt the pressure lift. "Without Comrade Xiaoping's understanding and backing," he said later, "I would not have passed the test since even Yaobang and Ziyang could not help me."

In May 1983, Guangdong provincial party committee and government delivered to the central committee a report on the crackdown on economic crimes, including smuggling and illegal peddling. The report said that, after the emergency notice of the central committee was implemented in 1982, a total of 7,675 cases of economic crimes had been recorded, investigated and handled, 4,768 cases had been concluded, more than 12,000 people were found to have been involved, including more than 5,300 party members and more than 4,800 state cadres, and that economic crimes were vigorously being tackled.

The storm was over at last and the situation of reform and opening up in Guangdong was maintained and continued to develop.

Chapter 25

Withstanding Pressure to Formalise Support for the SEZs

On 23 November 1980, Ren Zhongyi and Liang Lingguang headed for Shenzhen and Zhuhai SEZs. Most important, they found the senior leaders in Shenzhen to lack coordination. Highly experienced in local front-line work, Ren Zhongyi knew what it took to be an excellent and intrepid worker. He decided to change the leaders in Shenzhen, believing that the secretary of the provincial party committee, secretary of Shenzhen municipal party committee and mayor, Wu Nansheng, laid a solid

Ren Zhongyi (front row, third from right) and Liang Lingguang (front row, far right) visit Zhuhai SEZ, 25 November 1980

foundation for Shenzhen SEZ and transferred him back to the province to direct the work of the three SEZs. Ren Zhongyi and Liu Tianfu agreed that it was best to transfer Liang Xiang, member of the standing committee of Guangzhou provincial party committee and second secretary of Guangzhou municipal party committee, as Shenzhen's most senior leader. Through repeated negotiation, Liang Xiang finally agreed to accept this important mission. Ren Zhongyi selected and transferred from Guangzhou and other places a group of elite cadres who had both integrity and ability, and set up a highly competent leading group for Shenzhen SEZ. In February 1981, Liang Xiang enthusiastically took up his new post as first secretary of Shenzhen municipal party committee. Liang lived up to expectations, delivered an outstanding performance thanks to his courage and insight and set Shenzhen SEZ onto the fast lane of construction in little more than five years.

Ren Zhongyi (front row, third from right) accompanies the vice premier of the state council, Gu Mu, (front row, second from right) on a visit to Shenzhen SEZ

Ren Zhongyi (second from left) and Liang Lingguang (second from right) visit Shantou SEZ in the company of Wu Nansheng (third from left) and Fan Xixian (far right), November 1980

To speed up the development of Shenzhen SEZ, Ren Zhongyi proposed to have Shenzhen categorised as a municipality with independent planning status. Thanks to the efforts of Guangdong provincial party committee and Ren Zhongyi, the central committee approved the move and upgraded it to a sub-provincial city with Liang Xiang as vice governor, mayor and secretary.

Given the pioneering nature of the SEZs, many inlanders felt confused or doubtful, and some even had negative feelings about the SEZs. They claimed that they were inherently capitalist; others said "apart from the red flags, the SEZs have lost the sense of socialism"; some old cadres shed tears and said: "The hard work of decades has, overnight, been reduced to what existed before liberation." Ren Zhongyi and other provincial party committee leaders vigorously refuted the opinion that the SEZs were effectively turning back the clock to the era of concessions in China and argued strenuously to rehabilitate the good name of the SEZs.

"The sovereignty of the SEZs is in our hands," said Ren Zhongyi at a central work conference on 18 December 1980. "The government, police and army belong to us and they implement China's laws. What is the danger? There is no danger at all. Some ask whether the SEZs built on Chinese territory are not like the concessions in history. Those who worry about such things don't know the true situation. We build the SEZs for our interests only, rather than those of foreign countries. The economic cooperation of voluntary participation and mutual benefit is launched under the premise of not impacting on China's sovereignty. We share our interests with the economic partners for the sake of our own interests."

On 4 February 1981 (new year's eve), members of the Guangdong provincial party committee reported on the reform and opening up in Guangdong to Peng Zhen, secretary of the political and judiciary commission under the CPC central committee and vice chairman of the NPC, and Yang Shangkun, vice chairman and secretary general of the NPC. From left to right on the side of the table facing the camera: Liang Lingguang, Ren Zhongyi, Peng Zhen, Yang Shangkun, Liu Tianfu, Li Jianzhen and Wang De

He cited many facts to show the huge changes brought about by the SEZs. For example, the foreign exchange earned by Shenzhen from early 1980 to October 1980 was 1.7 times greater than for the whole of 1979, and was 1.8 times greater in Zhuhai over the same period. Zhuhai's fiscal revenues in 1980 were set to be 60% greater than in 1979. After the SEZs were built, the economy developed rapidly and people's lives were more colourful and diversified. He took the Shatoujiao (Sha Tau Kok) commune, separated from Hong Kong by a single street, as an example. The whole commune had a population of just over 1,300, with more than 2,600 having fled to Hong Kong since liberation. In recent years, an average of more than 120 people had fled to Hong Kong annually. But from 1979, the external flow rate started to fall. In 1980, none left at all and some of those who had been to Hong Kong returned. Most commune members built beautiful, western-style houses. Some said they lived better than the ministers of the central committee and the provincial governor. After the SEZs opened more to the outside world, more foreigners and Hong Kong and Macau compatriots came and went. However, the number of criminal cases declined and public security was even better than in some inland cities and towns.

Ren Zhongyi sees off Ye Jianying to Beijing at Guangzhou airport, 30 April 1981

At a Guangdong provincial party committee meeting on 18 May 1981, Ren Zhongyi pointed out: "Some comrades have concerns whether the SEZs constitute a loss of sovereignty, 'Hong Kongisation' or are in danger of becoming colonies. The answer is definitely 'no'. There is no precedent for an SEZ to become a colony. On the contrary, SEZs are built only when we have sovereignty. Running SEZs represents the application and exercise of sovereignty."

He listed six major advantages of the SEZs: to introduce more foreign capital, overseas Chinese capital, advanced technology and superior equipment; to better learn the advanced experience of foreign countries in operation and management and train local professional talents; to accumulate more foreign exchange, which is needed by the state for the four modernisations drive; to accelerate local modernisation of the SEZs; to provide references and experiences in the modernisation of the whole province and even the state; and, more significantly, to stabilise the opinions of the Hong Kong and Macau compatriots and expedite the peaceful reunification of Taiwan.

In the spring of 1982, Shenzhen municipal government allocated land to build Sino-foreign joint ventures and issued relevant local codes and regulations. Instantly, the public in inland regions seethed with indignation. "That guy Liang sold the land and sovereignty to foreigners," said some. "What a traitor." At that time, the central committee was launching an

Ren Zhongyi (front row, second from right) accompanies Wan Li (front row, third from right), vice premier of the state council, at a Chinese enterprise in Sha Tau Kok, Shenzhen, April 1981. Far right: Li Jian'an, vice governor of Guangdong province

anti-smuggling campaign. Shenzhen municipal party committee received *The Origin of the Concessions in Old China*, a white paper issued by a department of the central committee. Even Liang Xiang, who always dared to speak his mind and take action, kept silent, with his eyebrows knitted in a frown.

In June 1982, Ren Zhongyi travelled to Shenzhen SEZ with Chen Muhua, vice premier of the state council. Here, they are shown at an important railway line connecting Luohu port and Hong Kong. From the fourth from left: Liang Xiang, Chen Muhua, Wu Nansheng and Ren Zhongyi

Ren Zhongyi shakes hands with experts attending the first Guangdong SEZ seminar in Shenzhen, June 1982

In the piercingly cold month of February 1982, Ren Zhongyi, who was under huge personal pressure, went to Shenzhen three times in an effort to give the city and its leaders his full support: on 2 February, after the central committee issued an emergency notice; on 18 February, after Ren attended a meeting on the two provinces of Guangdong and Fujian; and on 6 March, after he delivered his second report in Beijing. Each time he met municipal party committee leaders, Ren did not criticise Shenzhen government but fully backed its achievements, urging it to quicken reform, relax policies, crack down on smuggling and to avoid politicising or exaggerating things, and encouraged all the leaders to stand up to pressure and apply themselves to the task of building the SEZs.

Ren Zhongyi accompanies the vice premier of the state council, Bo Yibo, on a visit to Zhuhai tourism centre in 1982

Each time Ren Zhongyi would have a separate discussion with Liang Xiang. On the third occasion, they talked privately for three hours. When the two shook hands in farewell, Liang Xiang felt a heavy burden lift from his shoulders, and he was filled with confidence. Afterwards, he led the leaders in devoting themselves to work with greater application. With the energetic support of Ren Zhongyi, Shenzhen had an unusual 1982. In late 1982, a theoretical expert from Beijing went to inspect Shenzhen. "The economic nature of the SEZs is not socialist," he said. "The SEZs should have their own attributes that are different from socialism. Otherwise, they would not be called SEZs… It is not suitable to define them as socialist." At a standing committee meeting of Guangdong provincial party committee on 25 April 1983, Ren Zhongyi refuted the view that the SEZs were not socialist. "The SEZs are built under the leadership of the party and the government and will never lose their sovereignty," he stated. "The establishment of the SEZs does not involve taking the capitalist road or jeopardising socialism, but instead will significantly benefit socialism."

In May 1984, Ren Zhongyi (front row, far right) accompanies a Yugoslav delegation headed by President Dragoslav Draza Markovic (front row, third from right) to visit a new housing estate for fishermen in Shenzhen SEZ. Liang Xiang is fifth from the right in the front row

Ren Zhongyi and Wang Xuan (far left) meet Deng Yingchao (far right), chair of the CPPCC on a visit to Shenzhen, December 1984

When he reported the work concerning the SEZs to Gu Mu in Guangzhou on 4 April 1983, Ren said: "I think the special policies for the SEZs should be continued. Vice Premier Wang Zhen told me in Hunan that some people have 'three fears' about SEZs – fear of Hong Kongisation, xenophobia and fear of bourgeois influence. Don't assume there is nothing good about 'Hong Kongisation'. The useful elements of 'soviet-plus-Hong Kong' can greatly enrich the communist movement."

After the visit, Gu Mu made a report to Deng Xiaoping in Beijing. On 25 June, Gu Mu passed on Deng Xiaoping's 15 June instructions: "The establishment of the SEZs should continue unswervingly. It is acknowledged at home and abroad that the SEZs have been built well and should continue in the future."

After that, the local people transformed Shenzhen from a small, remote fishing village into a bustling metropolis at the special 'Shenzhen tempo' in just a few years. One American marvelled that Shenzhen was a "city built overnight". Shenzhen created many firsts in China: the first to launch a programme of project tendering and bidding; the first to lease land; the first to implement pre-sales of commercial housing; the first to build a number of markets, including labour, raw materials, consumer goods, finance, technology, information, talent, futures and real estate. It created the 'Wanfeng model', a rural economic system of equity financing and participation based on public ownership and it became the first village nationwide to implement the stockholding system; built the first foreign exchange swap centre; built a storey of a building (Shenzhen International Trade Mansion) in the record time of just three days, which symbolised the Shenzhen tempo; took the lead nationwide to launch open recruitment of cadres at bureau level… Shenzhen's many successes were proof of the wise decision of the central committee to establish the SEZs and of the vigorous and effective leadership and support of Ren Zhongyi.

Willing Ox, a large sculpture in front of the gate to Shenzhen municipal government, symbolises the pioneering and reforming spirit of the Shenzhen people

Ren Zhongyi accompanies Hu Yaobang on a visit to a fishing village in Shenzhen, February 1983

Deng Xiaoping writes a complimentary message for Zhuhai SEZ, 29 January 1984

From 7 to 9 February 1983, Hu Yaobang, accompanied by Ren Zhongyi, You Taizhong and others, visited Shenzhen SEZ. "The SEZs are new things," he said. "You have delivered a good job to make innovation and achieved great things thanks to the efforts of the cadres." "You have blazed a new trail and perfectly achieved the goal of the central committee." From 23 to 24 May 1984, Hu Yaobang inspected Shenzhen SEZ again with Ren Zhongyi and Liang Lingguang and made the following impromptu inscription: "Handling special and new cases with special and new methods, with the stance unchanged".

From 24 January to 5 February 1984, Deng Xiaoping visited Shenzhen, Shekou, Zhuhai, Zhongshan and Shunde, witnessed the immense changes taking place in Guangdong after the opening to the outside world and wrote a tribute to Shenzhen SEZ: "The development and experiences of Shenzhen prove that it is a wise policy to establish the SEZs" and another message for Zhuhai SEZ: "Zhuhai special economic zone is good". Returning to Beijing, he said: "We establish the SEZs and implement the open policy under a guideline of opening to the outside world, in contrast to the close-door policy. The SEZs are a window of technology, management,

On 26 January 1984, Deng Xiaoping happily wrote the tribute "World on the Sea" with a brush for Shekou industrial zone

knowledge and foreign policy." In accordance with Deng Xiaoping's proposal, the central committee and the state council decided to open a further 14 coastal cities including Tianjin, Shanghai, Dalian, Guangzhou, Ningbo and Zhanjiang in April of the same year. Deng Xiaoping was in a cheerful mood when he met participants of the conferences on the work of some coastal cities. "The SEZs have grown to a formidable scale," he said. "It is an important precondition to select a leader who understands." These words were a resounding acknowledgement of the work and achievements of Guangdong and Ren Zhongyi.

Deng Xiaoping joyfully writes a tribute to Shenzhen SEZ in the Guangzhou Zhudao hotel. It reads: "The development and experiences of Shenzhen prove that it is a wise policy to establish the SEZs — 26 January 1984"

Later, an insider working alongside the central leaders said of Ren Zhongyi: "His major contribution was to have braved the enormous pressure and persisted in reform and opening up in adverse circumstances so that Comrade Xiaoping could see the practical achievements of the SEZs during his visit. If Comrade Zhongyi had not persisted in what he had done, he would have borne less pressure but nothing could later have proved the correctness of the reform and opening-up initiative and the establishment of the SEZs. If he had taken a step back, the inland regions would have regressed much further. Then the opponents would have said, with reason, that they had succeeded in eradicating what was wrong."

Chapter 26

'Giving Life' to Yuan Geng and Shekou Industrial Park

Shekou industrial park in the western part of Shenzhen was established in January 1979. Affiliated to the Ministry of Communications, it was the first pilot site of China's economic reform. Yuan Geng, managing vice president of the ministry's China Merchants Group, was the director of the industrial park's management committee. Courageous and knowledgeable, decisive and bold in action, he produced miraculous changes on what was a wasteland of only 2.14 square kilometres through arduous entrepreneurship.

Ren Zhongyi (third from right), Liang Xiang (fourth from right) and Yuan Geng (fifth from right) talk freely and cordially in Shekou industrial park, Shenzhen, 1986

Later, Yuan Geng recalled: "In a brilliant history of 10 years, Shekou has developed a different economic and political environment and has become a well-loved place. The achievements can be largely attributed to the support of the central committee and the provincial government. At that time, Hu Yaobang, Wan Li, Gu Mu, Hu Qili, Ren Zhongyi and Liu Tianfu showed unparalleled commitment to Shekou."

Shekou industrial park was a focus of controversy. Yuan Geng said that some companies had the power in their hands and would set up barriers if the old regulations were not followed by us whatever we said. To break away from the containment and intervention of bureaucratism and stereotypes, Yuan Geng repeatedly requested the central committee, the provincial government and the municipal government to give Shekou more autonomy. His requests were satisfied instantly during the tenure of Ren Zhongyi.

On 25 February 1981, Yuan Geng went to Guangzhou and reported the progress of Shekou industrial park's construction to the leaders of Guangdong provincial government, Shenzhen municipal government and the ministry of communications, and highlighted several problems needing urgent solutions. Ren Zhongyi said explicitly at the conference: Shekou industrial park had been built quickly and a summary of its construction experience was needed; the provincial party committee would offer its vigorous support and help to solve whatever problems were within its power; they would ask the central committee for solutions to the problems. Liu Tianfu backed Ren Zhongyi's view on behalf of the provincial government. Upon hearing of this support, Yuan Geng felt relieved at last.

The conference decided that: tax exemption would be applied to imported mechanical equipment, vehicles, raw materials and semi-finished products needed for the production and construction of the park, some daily necessities of the workers, and exported products and semi-finished products in Shekou industrial park; taxes would be reduced for imported cigarettes and alcohol sold in the industrial park; the industrial park should be surrounded with barbed wire and the park would be opened to foreign businessmen needing to enter and exit the park via Hong Kong to facilitate their access to Shekou; visas for foreigners did not need to be examined and approved by Shenzhen municipal government but in the industrial park by those who were dispatched by the provincial public security bureau; the right to manage an enterprise should be delegated and independent and autonomous operation and management should be implemented; the industrial park should be administratively led by the leaders of Shenzhen municipal government. Yuan Geng was satisfied with the outcome of the conference and was thankful for the support of Ren Zhongyi, Liu Tianfu and other Shekou leaders.

Ren Zhongyi accompanies Hu Yaobang in Shekou industrial park in Shenzhen, February 1983. Second row from left to right: Liu Tianfu, Hu Yaobang, Ren Zhongyi and Yuan Geng

In July 1984, Ren Zhongyi held a standing committee meeting of the provincial party committee, concluded that the committee and government approved the *Report on the Instructions to Solve the Problems of Shekou Industrial Park* of Shenzhen municipal party committee and government, and issued the No. 31 document of the CPC Guangdong provincial party committee. The document was of vital importance for Shekou because it specified the 10 major autonomies of Shekou industrial park including four governmental rights – the right of project approval, the right of examination and approval for imports and exports, the right of personnel administration and the right of management system reform. With such autonomy, Shekou industrial park could handle many affairs independently according to the needs of enterprises without requiring the time-consuming approvals of various levels. Shekou had the right to approve investment projects and make reporting and filing; it could approve permanent residency status for new employees and cadres; it could also daringly reform its management system. Additionally, the problem of the boundary between Shekou and Shenzhen was addressed.

Ren Zhongyi (far left) accompanies Chen Muhua (front row, far right) on a visit to Shenzhen's Shekou industrial park, June 1982. The person kneeling is Yuan Geng

Yuan Geng said later: "The No. 31 document was decided at the provincial party committee meeting presided over by Comrade Ren Zhongyi with the participation of the representative of Vice Premier Gu Mu on behalf of the central committee. The document properly handled the relationship between Liang Xiang and me, namely, the relationship between Shekou and Shenzhen, and enabled Shekou to become a genuine SEZ and a 'test tube of reform'."

The No. 31 document of the provincial party committee issued with the support of Ren Zhongyi, as Yuan Geng said, "gave life" to both him and Shekou industrial park. 'Giving life', in this context, meant 'bringing him to life' in Cantonese. The No. 31 document enabled Shekou industrial park to become the first place to really separate government administration from enterprise management in mainland China. It also explored an efficient new way to establish China's local authorities, cement the ability of Shekou to attract foreign capital and expand foreign trade, and to eliminate the barriers to system reform for Yuan Geng. Over time, Shekou became China's test tube of reform as Yuan Geng had predicted.

In January 1984, Deng Xiaoping inspected Shekou and was pleased with what he saw. "Shenzhen was built at a high speed," he said. "Shekou industrial park of Shenzhen developed faster thanks to its decision-making power. It can decide itself on projects costing less than US$5m."

Deng Xiaoping listens to Yuan Geng's report on his work in Shekou industrial park, 26 January 1984. Front row, from left: Liang Lingguang, Yuan Geng, Deng Xiaoping, Yang Shangkun and Wang Zhen

After the leading group of Shenzhen SEZ was adjusted, Ren Zhongyi felt that Liang Xiang carried a heavy burden in acting as both secretary of the municipal party committee and mayor. Therefore, he persuaded him to stay in charge of the municipal party committee while appointing someone else to take charge of the municipal government. Ren Zhongyi highly appreciated Yuan Geng's sterling efforts for reform and opening up in Shekou, along with his extraordinary intelligence, courage and adventurous spirit. After discussion, the provincial party committee decided to promote Yuan Geng to vice governor of Guangdong province and mayor of Shenzhen. It reported the promotion to the organisation department of the CPC central committee, which respected the view of Guangdong provincial party committee and approved Yuan Geng to take the two posts concurrently.

However, Yuan Geng was unwilling to take office and hurried to Beijing

'Giving Life' to Yuan Geng and Shekou Industrial Park

straight away. He said to Song Renqiong, director of the organisation department of the CPC central committee: "Shekou will collapse if I leave it now. I've worked in Shekou for years and it is about to succeed. Please consider withdrawing my new appointment." Song Renqiong said it was not the central committee that made the decision but the province that submitted the proposal, and advised him to discuss the matter with Ren Zhongyi.

Yuan Geng immediately took a plane to the provincial party committee and said to Ren Zhongyi: "The pilot reform in Shekou has just started up in a comprehensive way. I don't want to leave Shekou at this critical moment. Otherwise, my experiments in Shekou will not be completed." After deliberation and discussion with Liu Tianfu and others, Ren Zhongyi understood and approved Yuan Geng's requests and explained the situation to the central committee. The organisation department of the CPC central committee finally withdrew its appointment and fulfilled Yuan Geng's wishes.

Yuan Geng ordered a large sign to be erected, reading: 'Time is money and efficiency is life' at a crossing in Shekou industrial park, which immediately aroused great controversy

In this way, Ren Zhongyi helped 'give life' to Yuan Geng and Shekou industrial park. The whole country would later learn from the innovative reforms in Shekou. Yuan Geng proposed the slogan 'Time is money and efficiency is life', which won the support of Deng Xiaoping on his inspection tour and became a slogan of reform and opening up. Yuan Geng also implemented a merit-based recruitment mechanism, tried out 'ending the former rankings of cadres and adopting an appointment system' and applied a public selection and confidence vote system. The 'Shekou model' initiated pioneering reform of the personnel system. Yuan Geng managed the work of China Merchants Group for 14 years and increased its assets by up to 150 times from Rmb130m to Rmb20bn.

Yuan Geng asked Deng Xiaoping: "Does the slogan violate a taboo? We don't know whether we should take this risk. We don't require Comrade Xiaoping to give us a reply immediately. We only request we be allowed to continue with our practice and experiments." Deng Xiaoping, who gave his opinions only after careful consideration, uttered: "Very good"

In his late years, Ren Zhongyi praised Yuan Geng. "Yuan Geng is open-minded," he said. "The 'Shenzhen speed' to build Shenzhen International Trade Mansion primarily came from the 'Shekou speed'."

Chapter 27

'Eliminate Corruption, Not Outside Influences' to Solve TV Aerials Problem

After the conference on the work of the two provinces and the torrent of crackdowns on economic crimes in the first six months of 1982, Ren Zhongyi proposed what was to become a famous and well regarded slogan: 'Eliminate corruption, not outside influences'. The coining of this slogan came to signify Guangdong's policy of continuing to open up to outside influences.

From 1982, newspapers repeatedly mentioned Ren Zhongyi's slogan 'Eliminate corruption, not outside influences'

Ren Zhongyi heading a delegation to Macau with celebrated Hong Kong and Macau compatriots on 29 October 1981. Front row from left to right: Wang Kuang, Ke Zhengping, Ren Zhongyi, He Xian and Huo Yingdong. Second row from left to right: Li Jusheng, Liang Xiang, Ma Wanqi and Zeng Dingshi

The governor of Macau, Vasco Fernando Leotte de Almeida e Costa, meets Ren Zhongyi in the Macau government mansion, November 1981

'Eliminate Corruption, Not Outside Influences' to Solve TV Aerials Problem

In a media interview on 20 May 1982, Ren Zhongyi said: "We do not oppose everything foreign. It is wrong to do so. But we must eliminate corruption. The reform and opening-up policy has also brought some new problems. 'First come, first served' does bring advantages but it also means we will be the first to experience corruption. It is wrong and foolish to blindly reject foreign things; it is imperative and wise to actively eliminate corruption. A clear distinction should be drawn to identify real corruption. We should make specific analysis, summarise experiences, learn lessons and unify understanding."

As early as the group discussion of the central conference on 18 December 1980, Ren Zhongyi said: "Just as Comrade Wan Li said, we should focus on vital issues rather than trivial matters such as wearing bell-bottom trousers and long hair. Bourgeois corruption does not lie there but in the unhealthy trend of a minority of cadres taking bribes and engaging in embezzlement."

Ren Zhongyi holds a banquet in honour of Edward Fowler Hill, chairman of the Communist Party of Australia (Marxist-Leninist), and his wife Joyce in the Guangzhou Zhudao hotel, 19 April 1981

Between October and November 1984, Ren Zhongyi, in his capacity of adviser, visited Japan as a member of a CPC delegation headed by Qiao Shi (second from right), director of the organisation department of the CPC central committee. Here, Ren Zhongyi (far right) shakes hands with Akira Harada, vice general manager of Panasonic Corporation

Ren Zhongyi dines with Ezra Vogel, a famous China expert and Harvard professor, September 1988

'Eliminate Corruption, Not Outside Influences' to Solve TV Aerials Problem

Ren Zhongyi visits Shenzhen Dayawan nuclear plant under construction. The plant introduced advanced PWR nuclear power units from France

In a media interview on 19 September 1990, Ren Zhongyi reflected on the background to the slogan. "At that time, the central committee instructed a crackdown on all sorts of unlawful and criminal economic activities, such as smuggling and illegal peddling," he said. "Then, some raised doubts about the opening-up policy, leading to a sapping of confidence among some cadres. Against that background, the provincial party committee put forward the 'two unswervinglys' policy: unswervingly crack down on serious economic crimes and unswervingly continue with reform, opening up and economic invigoration. We do not blindly reject foreign things but should eliminate corruption actively. In brief, we should 'eliminate corruption, not outside influences'. It was proposed to focus on continuing with reform and opening up." "The stress was placed on not eliminating outside influences under the premise of eliminating corruption. Now, the emphasis must be laid on the elimination of corruption, not outside influences. It must be clear that the elimination of corruption must focus on two aspects – external corruption and internal corruption."

Thanks to Ren Zhongyi's adherence to the guideline of 'eliminating corruption, not outside influences', Guangdong's reform and opening up did not go the wrong way and managed to solve a major headache in the everyday life of Guangdong, the problem of proliferating television aerials, known as 'fishbone antennae'.

Ren Zhongyi (second from right) accompanies Gu Mu (far right) at a toy factory in the Pearl river delta featuring 'three-processing and one compensation'. Behind Ren is He Chunlin, director of the state council's SEZ office

'Fishbone antennae' dominate the view over the roofs of a rural area in the Pearl river delta

At the beginning of reform and opening up, Guangdong suffered a serious problem of 'fishbone antennae'. Families in coastal areas only needed to use bamboo poles to erect fishbone-shaped antennae with signal amplifiers over the roofs pointed in the direction of Hong Kong to directly watch television programmes broadcasted from Hong Kong. The colourful Hong Kong programmes were far more interesting than the dull, sermonising programmes on the mainland. In no time, fishbone antennae covered the roofs of Pearl river delta buildings like cobwebs.

The new Qiaobei area of Panyu, Guangzhou was densely covered with fishbone antennae like a bamboo forest

The fishbone antennae were denounced in mainland China. "Guangdong is being Hong Kongised and is becoming corrupt," said one high-ranking leader in public. A senior leader said: "When the fishbone antennae hang in the sky, the five-starred red flag will fall to the ground!" One department even described the nature of the phenomenon as 'reactionary publicity' and appealed that "it must be fought against and punished by law" and that the fishbone antennae must be dismantled. The central committee repeated its order to prohibit people from watching Hong Kong television programmes and said it was imperative to boycott the 'mental pollution' and corruption of bourgeois ideology.

Under pressure, Guangdong provincial party committee and government issued documents requiring cadres and party members not to watch Hong

Kong television programmes and to mobilise and educate the masses not to watch them also. The authorities dispatched working groups to all corners of the province and drove fire engines to forcibly dismantle the fishbone antennae. When they came to Guangzhou, the central leaders ordered high-powered jamming stations to interfere with the signals so that television screens across the whole Pearl river delta were dotted with snowflakes and fishbones.

When the central leaders came to Guangzhou, signals were jammed so that TV screens across the whole Pearl river delta were dotted with 'snowflakes' and 'fishbones'. A cartoonist satirises the development

But ordinary people still felt confused about matters. Before the working groups entered and the fire engines moved in, households rapidly took down their fishbone antennae only to erect them again in the evening. They were fed up with having to go through this exercise every day. Foreign businessmen were also unhappy: "What's the point of opening up if Hong Kong programmes are not allowed to be watched? How are we expected to do business? Where does our information come from?" The provincial party committee was perplexed about the problem.

After coming to Guangdong, Ren Zhongyi felt the matter had been handled poorly and would lead to more conflict between cadres and the masses, and also severely affect the long-term flow of foreign capital. At a central work conference on 22 December 1980, two months after he was transferred to work in Guangdong, Ren Zhongyi pointed out straightforwardly: "The problem of the masses in Guangdong watching

'Eliminate Corruption, Not Outside Influences' to Solve TV Aerials Problem

Hong Kong TV programmes is beyond government control. It's chiefly the result of the programmes of our own television stations being more rigid, fewer in number and less appealing. If our programmes are better, they wouldn't just be popular on the mainland, but Hong Kong people would set up their own fishbone antennae to watch them as well. It indicates that we should produce better and more appealing programmes. It is the most important and positive way out."

When Hu Yaobang came to Guangzhou and stayed in the Zhudao hotel in February 1983, the waiter was ordered to block all the Hong Kong television channels in the room. This is something that happened when all officials stayed at the hotel. Ren Zhongyi found out and immediately ordered these channels to be unblocked. He asked for the names of all these channels to be printed and placed beside the television set.

In the beginning of May 1983, Ren Zhongyi assigned Zhang Zuobin, deputy director of the publicity department of the provincial party committee, to check into a hotel in Shenzhen with his two assistants. They were tasked with noting all the Hong Kong television programmes for three consecutive days and nights and writing a survey report for Ren Zhongyi. The report showed that the television plays and variety shows of two Hong Kong channels were specifically aimed at ordinary Hong Kong people and were more interesting than the television programmes on the mainland that had just started. The intellectuals in Guangzhou generally liked news programmes, especially those transmitted by CNN and the BBC. CCTV did not broadcast such programmes and the news was often transmitted a day late. Hong Kong television programmes may have been occasionally vulgar and boring but they were not obscene and did not contain reactionary propaganda.

A few days later, Ren Zhongyi held a conference for the cadres in charge of publicity and culture in the publicity department of the provincial party committee and focused on two topics: first, to keep consistency with the central committee and not to advocate watching Hong Kong programmes; second, to produce our own wonderful television and radio programmes in order to diversify the cultural and entertainment lives of the people. He reaffirmed the importance of 'eliminating corruption, not outside influences' but added that it was totally wrong to throw the baby out with the bathwater by indiscriminately opposing foreign ideology and culture and blindly rejecting foreign things. He did not mention the problems of dismantling the fishbone antennae by force and interfering with the reception of Hong Kong channels.

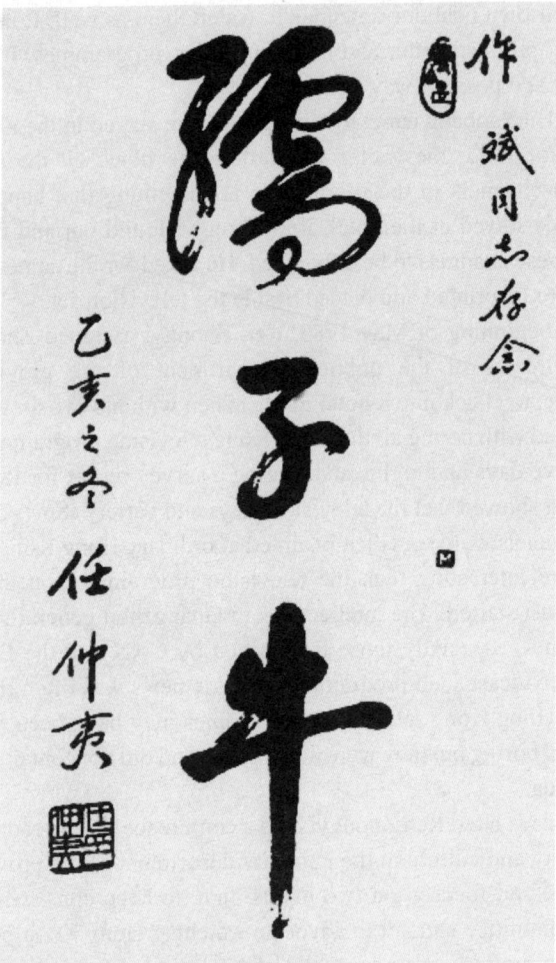

Ren Zhongyi wrote a message entitled *Willing Ox* for Zhang Zuobin, deputy director of the publicity department of the provincial party committee, to convey the view that cadres should conduct their business in the interests of the masses, just like a willing ox

He spoke on the issue of watching Hong Kong television programmes again at a standing committee meeting of the provincial party committee on 31 May. "First, party members should take the lead in refusing to watch such programmes," he said. "Second, the masses should be positively guided to watch our own programmes. Third, we should produce better programmes of our own, enrich their content, extend their broadcast duration and technically improve their visual effects." He still made no mention of dismantling the fishbone antennae by force or interfering with the reception of Hong Kong channels.

Ren Zhongyi and Li Ziliu talk cordially

On 24 May 1984, Hu Yaobang travelled via Shunde and asked Li Ziliu, secretary of CPC Shunde county party committee, for his views on Hong Kong television programmes. Li answered without reservation: "Mainland television programmes broadcast nothing but conferences and more conferences. But the Hong Kong programmes are lively and vivacious. News and live broadcasts are also available. As a matter of fact, positive thoughts are also broadcast, which plays a vital role in enabling people to get in touch with the outside world. We think it proper to handle the problem under the principle of 'eliminating corruption, not outside influences' proposed by provincial party committee secretary Ren Zhongyi."

From then on, during the tenure of Ren Zhongyi, Hong Kong television programmes were no longer interfered with and the fishbone antennae remained a unique feature of Guangdong through which each household could watch Hong Kong programmes in broad daylight.

Chapter 28

Invited by Henry Fok to Attend a Banquet at the White Swan Hotel

Built in 1979 with investment from the Hong Kong patriotic capitalist, Henry Fok, the White Swan hotel is a landmark building in Guangzhou. The hotel created many 'firsts' nationwide: It was the country's first five-star hotel involving foreign investment, the first large, modern joint venture to be designed, constructed and managed by China itself, the first hotel to make a profit in its first year of operation, the first hotel containing a Japanese-style restaurant co-run by Chinese, Japanese and Hong Kong parties, the first premium hotel with its four doors opened to welcome customers, the first hotel to deploy computerised management, the first hotel accepting payment by credit card and eight foreign currencies, and the first accepted as a member of the 'Leading Hotels of the World'. It was described by Hong Kong media as 'the first window of reform and opening up in Guangdong'.

The beautiful White Swan hotel was built on the north shore of White Swan lake

The 'hometown waterfall' in the hall of the White Swan

However, Henry Fok encountered unexpected resistance during the construction of the hotel. Up to 100,000 different types of products and materials were unavailable at that time on the mainland. To exacerbate matters, any imported items needed approval by up to 10 departments. Even more worrying was that anti-aircraft guns were set up on the roof of the White Swan as part of the city's military readiness. Henry Fok was dumbfounded: who would want to sleep in a place with artillery all around? He had no option but to turn to Ye Jianying for help in removing the air defence guns. He also wanted the hotel waitresses to wear silk stockings, which was regarded as an ideological problem. The female hotel staff who greeted customers at the gate of the hotel wore cheongsam and were described as a product of 'feudalism, capitalism and revisionism'. The hotel staff who wore kimonos in the Japanese-style restaurant were also criticised: "You traitors have brought in the ousted Japanese!" Henry Fok lamented with a sigh: "The White Swan hotel has so far brought me nothing but scathing criticism!"

Invited by Henry Fok to Attend a Banquet at the White Swan Hotel

The Yutangchunnuan Hall of the White Swan hotel was the location for Henry Fok's first banquet held in honour of Ren Zhongyi and other cadres when the hotel started trial operation on 14 October 1982

Ren Zhongyi brought more than 100 cadres to attend the trial opening banquet at the White Swan on 14 October 1982, which delighted Henry Fok

Between January 1984 and February 1985, Deng Xiaoping visited the White Swan three times. Here, Deng is warmly greeted by Henry Fok at the hotel

Ren Zhongyi (far right) accompanies Deng Xiaoping at the Guangzhou spring festival gala evening in the White Swan, 5 February 1984. Wang Zhen is second from left

Invited by Henry Fok to Attend a Banquet at the White Swan Hotel

To open the hotel as soon as possible, Henry Fok devised a plan to alleviate his problems and decided to begin trial operation one day before the start of the Guangdong autumn trade fair on 15 October 1982. He decided to invite Ren Zhongyi, first secretary of Guangdong provincial party committee, to the hotel that evening. In fact, he was not sure whether Ren could attend but he decided to make full preparations since the invitation had been sent out. He told the person in charge: "I've invited Secretary Ren Zhongyi to dinner. You should have the dishes well prepared, even if it is just four dishes and one soup." He also invited a group of Hong Kong chefs from the Zhucheng restaurant in Hong Kong in case those at the White Swan were not up to the task.

When he received the invitation, Ren Zhongyi was urged not to come: "If you go to this dinner, others will say you are mixing with capitalists and that you are sworn brothers." Ren Zhongyi responded: "Guangzhou and Hong Kong are not sworn brothers but full brothers who drink the same water from the Pearl river." He was not only glad to attend the dinner but also called on more than 100 provincial and municipal leaders to come along and show support for Henry Fok and the opening of the hotel. Their presence would also open their minds to the economic invigoration that was happening in the outside world.

When Ren Zhongyi led the group of cadres into the hotel, Henry Fok was truly taken aback. He hadn't expected so many of them to come, thinking perhaps two or three tables would be enough. In the event, more than 100 came and they were seated in the Yutangchunnuan banqueting hall.

He felt overjoyed later. After the guests took their seats, instead of being served four dishes and a soup, they were treated to 10 different cuisine styles elaborately cooked by the domestic chefs under the guidance of the Hong Kong experts. In total, more than 20 tables were served, not the planned two or three, which conveyed the scale of the banquet. Henry Fok felt great joy and excitement.

Henry Fok invited Ren Zhongyi to write a message for the White Swan hotel. Ren was happy to write: "Amid the constant sound of apes from both banks, the canoe has passed by thousands of mountains." This verse, laden with meaning, expressed not only Ren's praise and support for Henry

Fok but also his optimism for the reform and opening-up initiative in Guangdong and even the whole country.

On 6 February 1983, Henry Fok proposed the full opening of the White Swan. In the same way he invited Ren Zhongyi four months earlier, Fok sent a large number of invitation cards to the departments in charge of examination and approval in order to exert some pressure on them to handle the formalities and thereby enable the hotel to open. He succeeded again.

The success of the White Swan gave impetus to the injection of a large quantity of foreign capital into Guangzhou. Afterwards, a series of five-star hotels, including the China Grand, Garden and Oriental, opened for business in Guangzhou. Four of the five five-star hotels nationwide at the time were located in Guangdong, which precipitated the large-scale development of the hotel industry there.

Ren Zhongyi and Henry Fok take a boat to Guangzhou's Nansha development zone, invested in by Fok, 19 January 1999. Liang Lingguang is seated on the left

Invited by Henry Fok to Attend a Banquet at the White Swan Hotel

The success of the White Swan gave impetus to a large amount of foreign investment in establishing premium hotels in mainland China. This picture shows the opening celebration of the China Grand hotel in Guangzhou in 1984. Front row, from left to right: Hu Juewen (seated), Gu Mu, Ren Zhongyi and Wang Guangying

Chapter 29

Supporting Rural Hired-Labour Contracts in Specialised Households

At many conferences in Guangdong, Ren Zhongyi instructed that priority should be given in rural areas to "specialised contracting, the vigorous development of commodity production and socialised economic services". He also urged that more attention be paid to the issues concerning specialised contracting and that various types of 'specialised households' should be energetically fostered. At a conference for the secretaries in charge of agriculture of the prefectural and municipal party committees of the province on 18 June 1982, he said: "The responsibility system of specialised contracting not only reflects the principle of 'distribution according to work' but also promotes the concept of 'working according to one's ability' so as to give full scope to the technical expertise of individuals. There are capable brains and skilled workmen whose attributes have long been unknown and untapped in rural areas, and they have the chance to choose their tasks and play their roles, which will further emancipate productive forces."

With the development of rural economic reform in Guangdong and the support of the provincial party committee and government, a huge number of specialised households and economically capable brains came to the fore among farmers in pursuit of wealth. At that time, a heated debate was taking place regarding the permission for specialised households to hire labour and on the number of hired labourers. Like the permission for contracting, much of the focus was on whether it was socialist or capitalist. In the debate, Chen Zhixiong, a rich and influential farmer who was contracting a fishery and hiring labour, was condemned as a typical capitalist operator, which triggered nationwide debate.

Supporting Rural Hired-Labour Contracts in Specialised Households

Chen Zhixiong was a rich and influential farmer from Shapu commune, Gaoyao county, Zhaoqing city. His decision to hire labour triggered a nationwide debate

Chen Zhixiong was a farmer and expert fish-farmer in Gaoyao county, Guangdong province. The average yield ratio of his fishery per mu was 1.5-2 times higher than that of the local production team. He and his wife began to contract a 0.5-hectare collective fishery in 1979, expanded production in two production brigades and contracted 9.3 hectares of fishery in 1980. They were snowed under with work and hired one regular worker and several day labourers for a total of 400 work days. In 1981, he continued to expand the business and contracted 23.5 hectares. Another 9.3 hectares was sub-contracted to them by others through bidding. In addition to the work undertaken by him and his wife, Chen Zhixiong hired five regular workers and day labourers for a total of 1,000 work days.

The Gaoyao county party committee and Zhaoqing prefectural party committee had encouraged and supported Chen Zhixiong in his fishery's contract operation. In early 1981, the investigation team of the offices of the

Gaoyao county party committee and Zhaoqing prefectural party committee jointly wrote a *Survey on Chen Zhixiong's Contract Operation of More than 20-hectare Fishery* and held that his business "increased the revenues of the collective and the contractor". In February 1981, the general office of the provincial party committee circulated the investigation materials and comments to the provincial party committee leaders for reference. Having read them, Ren Zhongyi and Du Ruizhi, a member of the standing committee of the provincial party committee and director of the provincial agricultural committee, gave their full support. Ren Zhongyi thought such specialised contracting would play an active role in giving full scope to the technical expertise of commune members, in addition to improving fishery production and expanding the collective economy. He gave his written instructions that those places that satisfied certain conditions could start trial operation, summarise the resulting problems and make improvements.

Chen Zhixiong contracted 33 hectares of a fishery, hired five regular workers as well as day labourers for a total of 1,000 work days and became one of just two influential contractors nationwide, the other being Nian Guangjiu, the founder of Fool's Melon Seeds in Wuhu

However, Chen Zhixiong's practice of hiring labour touched a sensitive ideological nerve: can the hiring of labour, which has always been regarded as a sort of exploitation, be allowed to exist in a socialist country? Someone said it was capitalist exploitation and Chen was consequently put under stringent censure. It aroused uproar at the time. On 29 May 1981, *People's Daily* published a report headlined *Debate on Contracting of Fishery* on page two and featured a special column for discussion entitled *How to View Chen Zhixiong's Fishery Contracting*.

The 15 May 1981 edition of *Nanfang Daily* included an interview headed *Courage from Knowledge — Interview with Commune Member Chen Zhixiong Contracting Large Fishery*, which triggered a debate on the issue of hiring labour

Ren Zhongyi gave instructions on the investigation report on Chen Zhixiong's contracting of a large fishery and said that places satisfying certain conditions could start on a trial basis

The liveliest debate focused on whether labour hiring was exploitative. Those who agreed held the view that document No. 75 of the central committee in 1980 explicitly stipulated that the practice was strictly prohibited. Chen Zhixiong hired five regular workers and made profits not from individual labour but from labour hiring, which clearly showed the nature of capitalism. But the dissenters thought that Chen earned legitimate income through his own labour and operation, despite labour hiring, rather than through exploitation. An expert deduced from an analysis of the first volume of Karl Marx's *Das Kapital*: "Fewer than eight hired labourers are called helpers; if there are more than eight, they are regarded as being the victims of exploitation." For this reason, in China the figure of seven hired labourers became the strange but practical boundary line to distinguish between exploitation and non-exploitation.

Over three months, *People's Daily* published a total of 21 articles for debate and summarised the discussion in an article entitled *Further Emancipate Thinking About Economic Invigoration* on 30 August 1981. The article stated: "Chen Zhixiong is blameless for making more money primarily based on more pay for more work."

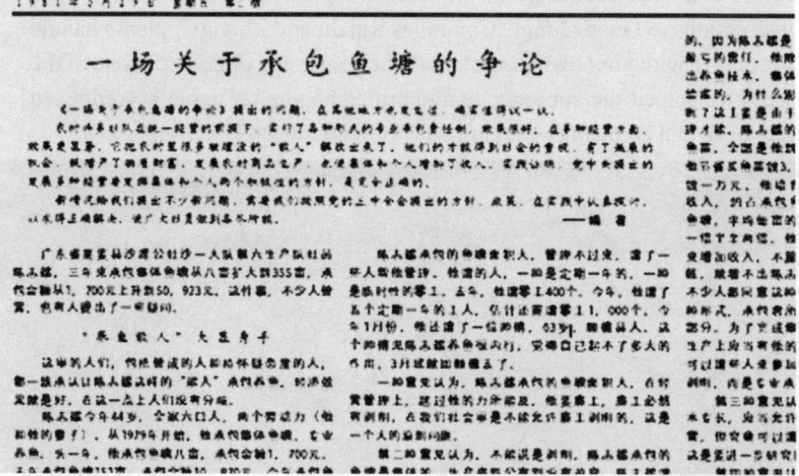

From 29 May 1981, *People's Daily* published an investigation report headed *Debate on Contracting of Fishery* along with a special column for discussion that was to run for three months entitled *How to View Chen Zhixiong's Fishery Contracting*

But the debate had still not been concluded by the end of this three-month period. A national meeting to discuss problems relating to the responsibility system for agricultural production in January 1982 issued an investigation report written by two participants from Guangdong Academy of Social Sciences' Institute of Economics, who went to make a field investigation of Chen Zhixiong's fishery and stressed that his business "was based on labour hiring rather than collective and unified operation. It has broken away from the responsibility system of the collective economy and has become a capitalist business. Restrictions should be imposed on it due to its disadvantages outweighing the advantages." "Chen Zhixiong's way of operation is no different from that [of capitalists] in the old society."

On 17 January, a correspondent from Xinhua news agency published an article based on the report entitled *Rich and Influential Contractors Based on Labour Hiring in Shapu Commune of Guangdong* for internal distribution, which aroused the close attention of central leaders. Hu Yaobang gave instructions later that day: "Comrade Runsheng, please pay attention to it and remind Guangdong provincial party committee of their need to act."

Two days later, Du Runsheng, director of the CPC rural policy research centre and deputy director of the national agricultural commission, gave instructions to Guangdong: "Comrades Ruizhi and Zhongyi, please handle the matter with your own discretion." The gentle and diplomatic tone of the wording helped the subordinate authorities handle the issue according to the facts. But some high-ranking CPC officials strongly censured it.

Ren Zhongyi (centre) in his later years, with Du Ruizhi (left), former member of the standing committee of the provincial party committee and director of the provincial agricultural committee, and Song Zhiying (right), former member of the standing committee of the provincial party committee and secretary of the provincial politics and law committee

Ren Zhongyi notified Du Ruizhi, a member of the standing committee of the provincial party committee in charge of agriculture and also director of the provincial agricultural committee, to promptly set up an investigation team of the provincial agricultural committee and go to Chen Zhixiong's fishery for investigation. On 22 April, the provincial party committee reported the investigation materials entitled *Report on Chen Zhixiong's Contract Operation* to the national agricultural commission. Based on the facts and reasoning, the report primarily affirmed that Chen Zhixiong set a precedent of specialised contracting that considerably benefited both sides of the arrangement. "The method of contracting and the way of operation are better than the past collective operation featuring 'egalitarianism' in terms of economic effectiveness yielded in the special historic conditions," it stated. Then, it refuted the statement of the two writers from Guangdong Academy of Social Sciences that "contracted business based on labour hiring" emerged in Shapu commune. It also proposed that "the problems in promoting the specialised contracted production responsibility system"… "should be settled after summarising the experiences and lessons and be guided and restricted in policy rather than by way of circulating a notice of criticism".

Ren Zhongyi firmly promoted the reform of the rural co-production contracting responsibility system in Guangdong. Here, he investigates the problem of the system in the poor county of Renhua in Shaoguan mountainous area in 1981. From right to left: Zhang Guoying, secretary of CPC Renhua county party committee, Ren Zhongyi, Ma Yipin, secretary of CPC Shaoguan prefectural party committee, and Yang Yingbin, member of the standing committee of the provincial party committee and secretary general of the provincial party committee

Chen Zhixiong's contract operation won the support of the provincial party committee and he continued to expand his business (later the efficiency declined due to over-expansion and poor management).

Guangdong provincial party committee and Guangdong provincial agricultural committee held a large conference on the problem of rural labour hiring and launched an extensive discussion on the advantages and disadvantages of the practice, the reasons for its emergence, the differences between labour hiring in two social systems and the prevailing strategies of labour hiring. A consensus was reached that the phenomenon of labour hiring was compatible with China's productivity level in the initial stage of socialism; it was good for increasing output thanks to the advantages outweighing the disadvantages; it was advisable to make the best use of the circumstances to promote the benefits and minimise the drawbacks rather than adopt forcible administrative measures to curb the practice. The publication of the minutes of the conference and the main theses in the Beijing newspapers generated positive influence nationwide. Thanks to the unequivocal response of Ren Zhongyi and other leaders to fully affirm and encourage the rich and influential contractors to hire labourers without prohibition, specialised rich and influential rural contractors sprang up like mushrooms.

Ren Zhongyi repeatedly praised the specialised rural households. At a Guangdong award ceremony for specialised households on 26 September 1984, he said: "Specialised households are the pioneers of common rural prosperity, the representatives of advanced rural productivity, the activists of rural economic reform and the new farmers of socialism." "Specialised households are the new products of rural development that deserve the care, protection and active support of party committees and governments at all levels. All departments and all industries should offer their support for specialised households."

Deng Xiaoping took a measured response in a speech on 22 October 1984. "The problem of labour hiring caused a major vibration that aroused our deep concerns," he said. "I think we should wait and see its effect after two years. Will it affect our overall situation? If any new measures are adopted, the masses will think the policies are changed and they will feel uneasy. If Fool's Melon Seeds [a company founded by Nian Guangjiu in Wuhu, Jiangsu province] is suspended from operation, the people will not rest assured. There is no point in doing it. Let Fool's Melon Seeds operate for a period of time. Is there anything wrong in that? Will it be harmful to socialism?"

On 27 May 1982, Ren Zhongyi (far right) and Liu Tianfu (second from right) went to a rural area in Huaiji county, Zhaoqing to assess the local floods and labour hiring of specialised households. Seated far left is Guo Rongchang, secretary of the provincial party committee and secretary of CPC Zhaoqing prefectural party committee

Ren Zhongyi and Guangdong provincial party committee offered an opportunity for the labour-hiring policy of specialised households, which had a significant impact on the future of private enterprises and gave them room to operate and develop. By 1985, when Ren Zhongyi left office in Guangdong, private enterprises in the Pearl river delta had hired 5m workers who, together with the millions of wage earners in the three kinds of investment enterprises, sparked the first round of the massive influx of peasant workers. Since then, Guangdong has always had more migrant peasant workers than any other province, accounting for about 30% of the national total. They have invigorated the local economy and brought in a new model of development.

Chapter 30

Guangdong Becomes National 'Pacesetter' of Reform and Opening Up

Between 1981 and 1985, when Ren Zhongyi administered Guangdong, the provincial party committee firmly and correctly implemented the special policies and flexible measures granted by the central committee, took the first step nationwide, brought earthshaking and radical change to the province and produced many important nationwide firsts.

Guangdong completed the targets of the sixth five-year plan one year in advance. Its gross output value of industry and agriculture rose by 13.7% and national revenue jumped by 11.7% annually on average over the five years, surpassing the figures for any previous period. The total value of the economy, which had long remained backward, leapt to among the top three nationwide during the five years, reached the number one position three years later, accounting for one-eighth of the national total, and has ranked first nationwide ever since.

Cartoon - *Ren Zhongyi: Braving the Rugged Road Ahead*

Ren Zhongyi visits a recuperating Xi Zhongxun in Shenzhen and the two reformers shake hands warmly, 7 February 1997

In January 1992, Deng Xiaoping visited Shenzhen and Zhuhai in the hope that Guangdong would accelerate its development and lead China's push in catching up with Asia's 'four little dragons' in 20 years. Under the leadership of the central committee and thanks to the promotion of reform pioneers such as Xi Zhongxun and Ren Zhongyi, Guangdong's GDP surpassed that of Singapore in 1998, Hong Kong in 2003 and Taiwan in 2007. GDP growth surpassed that of South Korea in 2005, while total GDP almost reached the level of South Korea in 2012, matched it in 2013 and was expected to surpass it in 2014.

Guangdong was the first province to make breakthroughs in pricing and reforming the production and marketing system of farm produce. When Ren Zhongyi took office, consumers had to use coupons to purchase 46 types of daily necessities, including soup, cigarettes and matchsticks. After analysing the situation, Ren decided to take the lead in reforming the purchase and sale systems for agricultural byproducts such as vegetables, fish and fruit, before also including industrial and consumer products and then production materials. When he took office in November 1980,

Guangdong decided to implement a production and purchasing policy of incentives for overproduction of sugar cane and grain tonnage to boost output of cane sugar. In December of the same year, Guangdong authorities decided to reform the grain work system and implement grain and oil purchase and sale on a contract basis. From 1981 to 1983, Guangzhou was the first to successively open the pricing for agricultural byproducts, made remarkable achievements despite several ups and downs and stirred up a nationwide reaction. In 1983, the prices of almost all agricultural byproducts were opened in Guangdong. In just three years, the empty store shelves in Guangzhou had become crowded with a wide variety of commodities. A brisk market, Guangzhou suddenly became a shopping paradise nationwide. In 1984, Shenzhen SEZ took the lead in opening a grain market, eradicating the state monopoly on the purchase and marketing of grain and oil, and comprehensively implementing negotiated purchasing and selling, as well as unlimited supply. In 1985, the whole province eradicated the policy of prescribed state purchase quotas for farmed fish and live pigs. The successful pricing breakthrough in Guangdong provided the rest of the country with an example of price reform and the establishment of an agricultural products market mechanism.

Guangdong was the first province in China to reform its financial system. From 1981, it implemented a new fiscal system featuring divided responsibility and tiered revenue and expenditure in all cities and counties except Guangzhou, Shenzhen, Zhuhai and Hainan. The system of dividing revenue and expenditure between the central and local governments gave local authorities greater autonomy, mobilised the enthusiasm of all levels of local government to manage monetary affairs, raise revenues and reduce expenditure, and expedited productivity improvements.

Guangdong was the first nationwide to implement the contract system of inviting bids for projects. In January 1981, Shenzhen took the lead in an important reform to building engineering construction. China First Metallurgical Construction won the open bidding for an international commercial building project in Shenzhen. Construction costs were reduced by 22% and the construction time was halved from two years to one year.

Ren Zhongyi and Governor Liu Tianfu, close comrades-in-arms, in front of Daban rock in Fengkai county, Zhaoqing in 1982

Guangdong was also the earliest to reform the construction investment system along the lines of 'borrowing chickens to hatch eggs'. Ren Zhongyi thought it was not feasible to carry out construction simply by means of fiscal appropriation and instead urged the participation of all social elements in investment to mobilise all the social elements to participate in investment. So he put forward the principle that 'whoever invests receives the profits'. Guided by this idea, Guangdong raised funds for infrastructure projects and maintained them with the returns from such projects and fundamentally addressed the problem of inadequate transportation that had burdened the province for so long. In only a few years, investment in roads from all sources in the province amounted to tens of billions of renminbi. The funds were used to construct and reconstruct some 5,000km of highways, to resurface 5,000km of highways, to build more than 1,000 roads and bridges, and to build 1,000km of first- and second-class highways and expressways. In only a couple of years, Guangdong completed the construction of hundreds of wharfs and dozens of 10,000-ton deepwater berths. The cargo-handling capacity of Guangdong's ports rose rapidly by million of tons and accounted for 20% of the national total. Gross imports and exports at its foreign trade ports made up nearly half of the national total, surpassing the combined total of more than 20 major ports such as Qinhuangdao, Yantai, Qingdao, Tianjin, Shanghai, Ningbo and Xiamen. By starting its own company, issuing bonds and borrowing from banks, Guangdong railway was able to build, in just a few years, the Hengyang-Guangzhou double-tracked railway line, the Guangzhou-Shenzhen double-tracked line, the Sanshui-Maoming railway and the Guangzhou-Meizhou-Shantou railway that established a connection to Fujian. In January 1984, the first independent economic entity of the national railway system – Guangshen (Guangzhou Shenzhen) Railway Company – was founded, breaking through the traditional organisational model and implementing an economic contracting management system featuring independent operation, sole responsibility for its own profits and losses, self-improvement and integrated self-development.

The leaders of the SEZs including Ren Zhongyi (centre), Liang Xiang (second from right), secretary of CPC Shenzhen municipal party committee and mayor of Shenzhen, Liang Guangda (second from left), secretary of CPC Zhuhai municipal party committee and mayor of Zhuhai, and Huang Jing (far right), deputy secretary of CPC Zhuhai municipal party committee

Guangdong Becomes National 'Pacesetter' of Reform and Opening Up

Ren Zhongyi accompanies Deng Xiaoping at a spring festival gala evening for Guangzhou soldiers and civilians, February 1984

On 19 February 1999, Ren Zhongyi and his wife arrive in Shenzhen to visit Xi Zhongxun and his wife. From left to right: Wang Xuan, Ren Zhongyi, Xi Zhongxun and Qi Xin

The inaugural Guangzhou book fair, the first of its kind nationwide, was held in Guangdong in June 1981 where more than 10,000 types of books from 103 publishing houses were displayed.

Hu Yaobang and Ren Zhongyi in Guangzhou in February 1983

Comrade Jiang Zemin pays a cordial visit to Ren Zhongyi in February 2004

Guangdong was the first nationwide to accept overseas donations to establish universities. In August 1981, the province accepted a donation from Hong Kong compatriot Li Ka-shing to establish Shantou University, which was completed in 1990.

The SEZs in Guangdong took the lead in lawmaking throughout the country. In December 1981, the standing committee of Guangdong provincial people's congress, as authorised by the standing committee of the NPC, released four items of separate laws and regulations relating to the SEZs in Guangdong including *Temporary Provisions on Management of Entry-Exit Personnel in Guangdong SEZs* and *Temporary Provisions on Management of Enterprise Labour Wages in Guangdong SEZs*.

Guangdong was the first to reform the land-use system in China. In December 1981, the *Temporary Provisions on Land Management in Shenzhen SEZ* began to implement the paid state-owned land-use system and levy land-use fees from foreign businesses.

From left to right: Li Peng, Jiang Zemin, Ren Zhongyi, Li Ruihuan and Liu Huaqing at the party's 16th National Congress

During a visit to Guangdong, General Secretary Hu Jintao pays a visit to Ren Zhongyi at Ren's home, April 2003

Li Ruihuan, CPPCC chairman, visits Ren Zhongyi in Guangzhou, 2002

Guangdong Becomes National 'Pacesetter' of Reform and Opening Up

Ren Zhongyi and Comrade Li Changchun at the ninth Guangdong party congress, May 2002

Ren Zhongyi and Comrade Zhang Dejiang at the fifth plenary session of Guangdong's ninth party congress, September 2004

Ren Zhongyi and Comrade Wang Qishan at the Guangdong provincial people's congress, 1998

Ren Zhongyi talks with Comrade Zhang Gaoli, 22 May 1998

Guangdong was the first province in China to initiate the process of rural industrialisation. From 1979, it began to introduce 'three-processing and one compensation' enterprises (enterprises that: process imported raw materials for their clients; assemble imported parts for clients; and manufacture products according to clients' samples; then repay loans for imported equipment and technology in kind with products). In 1981, the Pearl river delta developed a great number of foreign-owned enterprises, township enterprises and private enterprises. In 1985, the 'four little tigers' development model was formed in Guangdong: the Dongguan model took foreign capital investment as the main measure, processing trade as the breakthrough and the export-oriented economy as the direction; the Shunde model and the Zhongshan model prioritised the development of township enterprises and local private capital gradually played a leading role after the reform; the Nanhai model integrated state-owned, collective and private economies and gave full play to the counties, communes, production brigades, production teams, private enterprises and consortia. These typical county economic development models rapidly realised industrialisation and attracted the world's largest rural labour population on the path of state industrialisation, modernisation and urbanisation. Sociologist Fei Xiaotong summarised them as the 'Zhujiang model' (Pearl river model), which was known as one of the three major paragons of industrialisation, modernisation and urbanisation in the early stage of China's reform and opening up together with the south Jiangsu model and the Wenzhou model.

In early 1982, the first generation of China's young migrant job-hunters emerged in Guangdong, which became the most popular destination for migrant workers nationwide and led to the first wave of peasant workers in China.

In January 1982, the Shenzhen branch of Nanyang Commercial Bank, the first foreign-funded bank introduced to mainland China, started business.

The nation's first initial public offering (IPO) by a corporate enterprise was launched in Guangdong. On 8 July 1983, the first share of a corporate enterprise in the history of the new China was publicly issued by Bao'an County Joint Venture Corporation in Shenzhen and the first mainland corporate enterprise, Shenzhen Bao'an Joint Venture Corporation, came into being.

In January 1983, the personnel department of Guangdong government took the lead in setting up the first human resources organisation in China. In November, the Guangdong foreign talent recruitment leading group office was set up.

Ren Zhongyi, Wan Li, Yang Shangkun and Xie Fei in Guangzhou, 3 March 1994

China's labour contract system was first promoted in Guangdong. In March 1983, the provincial government approved the labour contract system in recruitment, introduced a policy to break the 'iron rice bowl' of guaranteed job security and took the lead in establishing the labour contract system and the employee pension insurance system in June of the same year.

The first law firm in China was founded in Guangdong. In July 1983, Shenzhen Shekou Industrial Zone Legal Services Company set up shop and opened for business.

China's first four-tier twin-ring intersection was built in Guangzhou. In December 1983, the Guangzhou Quzhuang intersection was put into service and was awarded first prize for scientific and technological progress in a competition run by the ministry of construction in 1985. Ren Zhongyi made on-site inspections and instructions during its construction.

In 1983, Guangdong was the first province to invest huge sums of loans in civil aviation in the name of the local government, which broke through the existing practice whereby the civil aviation administration of China (CAAC) bought planes and allocated them to airlines.

Guangzhou was the first to break the unified wage model in China. In August 1984, Guangdong provincial government approved a plan to reform the wage system of government offices and public institutions in Shenzhen. The wage structure in Shenzhen SEZ was divided into basic, duty and seniority wages after the reform.

The most advanced and largest microwave reversible link dedicated to radio and television broadcasting was completed and put into service in the Pearl river delta in August 1984, serving Guangzhou, Shenzhen and Zhuhai.

Guangdong provincial education broadcasting station, the first of its kind at the provincial level nationwide, officially went on air in September 1984.

The first sports team to be jointly operated by an enterprise and an athletics committee was established in Guangdong. Guangzhou football team was jointly set up by Baiyunshan Pharmaceutical general factory and Guangzhou sports committee in October 1984. The team came to be known as Guangzhou Baiyun.

The earliest centralised government affairs organisation in China was established in Guangzhou. In January 1985, an organisation specially handling foreign trade and economic affairs was set up in the Guangzhou Oriental hotel, and was known as 'foreign trade and economy street' for short. Offices of the administrative units relating to foreign trade and economics, industry and commerce, taxation, administration, labour, banking, law, insurance and customs were built in the street in a centralised way to help foreign businesses pass the formalities.

Guangdong provincial land bureau, China's first provincial-level management organisation to unify the management of urban and rural land in an area, was officially established in June 1985.

Guangdong took the lead in setting up comprehensive reform experimental units in China. In May 1985, comprehensive economic reform experimental units were built in Guangzhou, Foshan, Jiangmen and Zhanjiang. In November 1987, the state council decided to make Guangdong a comprehensive reform experimental district.

Ren Zhongyi talks with Ye Xuanping, vice chairman of the CPPCC and former governor of Guangdong at a group discussion conference of the 15th congress of the CPC, September 1997

Guangdong also produced many other nationwide firsts during Ren Zhongyi's administration, which significantly promoted reform and development in the province, accumulated experience for the reform and development of the country, and explored the way ahead. Guangdong really took the first step in reform and was the pacesetter of reform and opening up in China. All the achievements in Guangdong during his administration were deeply imprinted with the name Ren Zhongyi and he will always be synonymous with reform and opening up in Chinese history.

Chapter 31

Performing Official Duties Honestly and Never Giving Personal Favours

Always cherishing the values of people's supremacy, Ren Zhongyi considered how to make the people become more prosperous economically, exercise more political democratic rights as masters of the state and enjoy more success in cultural and spiritual civilisation. A government official of 70 years, he never claimed credit for himself or became arrogant, nor did he think about his own losses or gains or ask organisations to give him preferential treatment. Any special treatment that he did deserve was given to others, which showed his wholehearted devotion to public duty.

Ren Zhongyi and Wang Xuan at Jingpo lake in Heilongjiang, 1973

Ren Zhongyi and Wang Xuan in Shenyang in 1978

The house in Guangzhou where Ren Zhongyi lived had for decades been the residence of officials in charge of the provincial party committee and no one had proposed any change to that arrangement. After he was transferred to Guangdong, Ren Zhongyi knew about the problem of insufficient housing for the provincial party committee. Although it was not spacious for the three generations of his family, Ren Zhongyi still actively requested to reconfigure the house and courtyard and share half of it with others before he left office as first secretary of the provincial party committee in 1985. The housing management cadres of the provincial party committee tried to persuade him not to change it and the authorities wanted to look for alternatives. But he insisted on splitting the house into two parts and his family proceeded to live in one half while the other half was allocated to another household.

"Generally, as leaders are promoted, they tend to live in larger houses," said one cadre. "Secretary Ren was the single exception, especially before he left office. Far from asking for a bigger house, he actually returned the house, which deserved our high admiration." State President Yang Shangkun went to Ren Zhongyi's house in Guangzhou to see him without advance notice. Comrade Yang Shangkun had once lived in the house and, finding it too small, he asked the reasons and highly praised what Ren Zhongyi had done.

Ren Zhongyi never used his power to give favours to his family or relatives and refused to give preferential treatment to his family and friends. His wife, Wang Xuan, was a veteran cadre who hurled herself into the revolution during the December 9 movement and she was as senior as him. She worked as deputy director of the former organisation department of Songjiang provincial party committee and deputy director of the provincial personnel bureau as far back as 1952. She took office as deputy director of Harbin revolutionary committee (equivalent to vice mayor) in 1972. The municipal party committee proposed to admit her into the leading group of the municipal party committee according to her ability, experience, performance and seniority. But Ren Zhongyi thought his wife should serve as a good example of honest governance. He asked her to cede the position to another. Serving the interests of the whole, she refused to work as a leader of the standing committee of the municipal party committee.

Ren Zhongyi and Wang Xuan in Guangzhou in 1981

Ren Zhongyi and Wang Xuan on the Tiananmen tower in the autumn of 1987

In the spring of 1977, Ren Zhongyi was transferred to work in Liaoning and Wang Xuan became deputy mayor of Shenyang. The municipal party committee proposed she worked as a leader of the committee but Ren Zhongyi disagreed. In November 1980, Ren Zhongyi was transferred to administer Guangdong. Beijing municipal party committee proposed that Wang Xuan be appointed deputy mayor of Beijing and prepared a house for her. But Ren Zhongyi wanted her to join him in Guangzhou. To support her husband, Wang Xuan resolutely, and without regret, gave up the post of deputy mayor of Beijing and worked as deputy mayor of Guangzhou, a city with a lower ranking than the national capital. During her tenure in Guangzhou, the municipal party committee proposed to Ren Zhongyi to admit Wang Xuan into the leading group of the standing committee of the municipal party committee, which he refused. Soon afterwards, the leading organisation of Guangdong province needed a female leader and some leaders of the provincial party committee said that Wang Xuan merited the position because of her rare seniority and capability. But Ren Zhongyi thought it improper to work in the leading organisation of the provincial level together with his wife and that she should render services in Guangzhou municipal government, which was a secondary leading organisation. He persuaded the leading group of the provincial party committee not to promote Wang Xuan. She understood her husband's motive and gave up the promotion. Her position remained the same until her retirement, working at the rank of deputy mayor, either in Harbin, Shenyang or Guangzhou. However, she did not voice any complaint.

Just before he died, Ren Zhongyi repeatedly told his sons: "You should take good care of your mother. She is strong-minded and sensible. I will rest assured if you can look after her well." 'Considerate and reasonable' mainly referred to her understanding and support for his decision to block her promotion time and again.

It is incredible that Ren Zhongyi did not arrange for a single relative to work in Guangzhou and that even his younger sister and younger brother had never even visited Guangdong during his 25-year administration.

Ren Lantian, younger brother of Ren Zhongyi

Two representatives, Ren Zhongyi and Ren Kelei, father and son at the ninth congress of party representatives of Guangdong, held in Guangzhou. Ren Kelei was elected as a party representative not because he was a son of Ren Zhongyi but for his excellent work record in Guangdong

Ren Zhongyi was a man who cherished family affection and had been on good terms with his younger sister Ren Yurong and younger brother Ren Lantian. When he returned to work in Liaoning in August 2003, he spared some time to visit his younger brother living in Xiongyue town, Gaizhou county, Liaoning. Lantian was a retired agronomist with a thorough knowledge of Ren Zhongyi's character and his refusal to grant privileges to family and friends. So he never requested any personal favour or gained any advantage from his brother while he held the post of first secretary of Liaoning provincial party committee. The four generations of the family were squeezed into a house of about 60 square metres where it was often difficult to find somewhere to sit down or turn around. On the day of their meeting, Ren Zhongyi said: "Lantian, I worked in Guangdong for more than two decades. But you've never been there. I hereby invite you and your wife to enjoy yourselves in Guangdong next spring and let's have a good time there." Lantian agreed with heartfelt delight.

At lunch time, he invited his younger brother to a restaurant. But it was the party regulation that the only participants should be Lantian, his wife and their sons, with the others having to eat at home. His secretary suggested he should invite all the family members of his younger brother. "How can I?" he retorted. "If I invite that many people to lunch, it will not only generate bad feelings but also bring trouble to the organisation."

Ren Zhongyi visits his younger sister Ren Yurong in Xingtai, Hebei, accompanied by his son Ren Kening, 1980

The following spring, Ren Zhongyi did not forget his appointment with his younger brother, and invited Lantian to Guangdong. However, due to the poor health of Lantian's wife, the trip never happened. When Ren Zhongyi invited him to Guangdong in the autumn, Lantian fell ill and could not travel. In the third year, Ren Zhongyi himself was hospitalised and then passed away. The holiday between the brothers never happened.

Ren Zhongyi meets up with his younger sister in Xingtai in the autumn of 1986

Ren Zhongyi wrote a message for his younger sister Ren Yurong

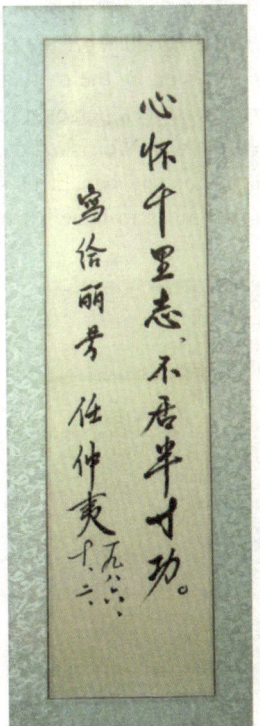
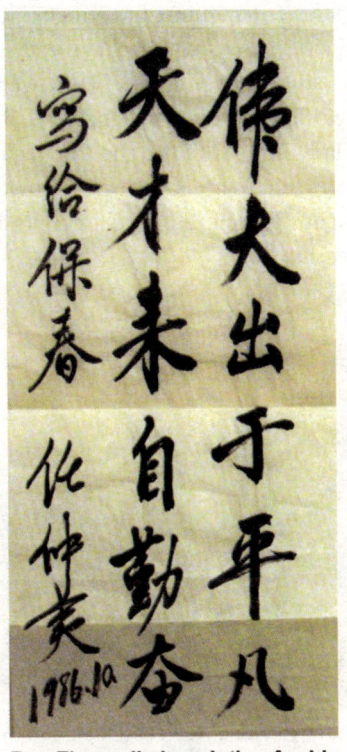

Ren Zhongyi's inscription for his niece Luo Lifang

Ren Zhongyi's inscription for his niece Luo Baochun

Ren Zhongyi liked his younger sister very much. As a child, when he returned to his hometown with his father, he often held Yurong's hand, sat on a grain stack in a field, gazed at the moon and told her stories full of family affection. Before he was transferred to work in Guangdong in 1980, he spared time to see his younger sister in Xingtai after an absence of 35 years. Following that, he went to Xingtai to see her on five occasions. When colleagues of his nephews and nieces knew that they had such an illustrious uncle, a high-ranking official, they said: "It's foolish of you not to make the most of such a useful relationship. Why don't you ask your uncle to put in a good word for you with your superiors?" Their mother always replied: "Don't turn to your uncle. I know him too well. It would be useless. Don't cause trouble for your uncle."

Whenever he returned to Xingtai, Ren Zhongyi would tell his nephews and nieces: "You should behave yourself and do a good job. Don't expect to gain advantage from me. My power was entrusted by the party and the people. I have no right to handle personal affairs or seek personal gain for my relatives. Your father and I both survived the war. We risked our lives in revolution. Who could ask the organisation for any benefit or special treatment? Therefore, you should not have any plans to benefit from our relationship."

Ren Zhongyi, Wang Xuan and their son Ren Kening, together with Zhang Yueqi and Lei Yu, husband and wife, In 1988

Ren Zhongyi celebrates his 90th birthday with former staff members, September 2004

A family photo of Ren Zhongyi, Wang Xuan, their sons, daughters-in-law, grandson and granddaughter in Gongbei, Zhuhai during the spring festival of 1987

When Ren Zhongyi returned to Xingtai on national day in 2004, Yurong had been dead for nine years. He said to his nephews and nieces: "I've never helped my relatives gain personally from my work over so many years, so family members and others say I have severed old ties. They said it! I have no power to do any personal favours for you. It's no use complaining about it. Whoever it is, even my own son, I will not get involved"

Ren Zhongyi, Wang Xuan, their eldest grandson Ren Ge and his wife and their great-grandson

Ren Zhongyi picks a bunch of wild flowers at the foot of Yulong snow mountain, Lijiang, Yunnan province for his life-long beloved wife Wang Xuan, August 1998

Traditional Chinese painting *Red Kapok Tree in Wind and Rain (Governor of Guangdong through Trials and Hardships)* by Sun Ge

After Ren Zhongyi passed away, his niece Luo Lifang wrote emotionally in his memory: "It was his refusal to grant privileges to his family and friends that highlighted his honest governance, exemplary conduct and nobility of character not swayed by personal conditions in his work. However, he was always generous to the less fortunate and he donated Rmb100,000 to his hometown to establish Hope primary schools so that the local children could attend school. For decades and right to the end of his days, he exerted his utmost effort to perform his duty. My uncle did not cut loose from his family and friends. The great motherland and the people are his closest family and friends."

When he visited a veteran cadre activity centre in Dalian on National Day in 1985, Ren Zhongyi was invited to write a message. He encouraged other veteran cadres by writing: "Cherishing far-reaching ambition in heart without claiming any credit". Actually, the message was an accurate depiction of Ren in retirement and, indeed, perfectly depicted his whole life.

Epilogue

Ren Zhongyi passed away in Guangzhou on 15 November 2005 at the age of 92.

His death aroused strong reaction in society. People expressed their mourning for him. Domestic and overseas media made repeated references to and highly evaluated his lifelong achievements.

Ren Zhongyi devoted his whole life to reform and never gave up or kept silent on this issue. In his later years, he still paid much attention to political, economic and cultural reform and exerted all his energy to support the reforms with his profound thoughts, intrepid courage, incisive writing style and wise words. His piercing and pertinent understanding of the reform process and his persistent action stood out among the whole party and the whole country.

Ren Zhongyi said in his twilight years: "I had my gallbladder removed in November 1983. Despite losing this organ, I was filled with courage and strength, and feared nothing. In November 1993, at the age of 80, I had four-fifths of my stomach cut out. I did not care a scrap and feared nothing." In January 1985, he suffered from aphasia, a speech and language disorder that resulted from cerebral apoplexy. But he took great pains to practise speaking and recovered more than 80% of this facility in just over six months. "I recovered my speech from God," he joked. He was diagnosed with bladder cancer in November 2001, heeded the advice of doctors after the surgery and achieved a remarkable recovery. "Congratulations on your victory" he told the doctors later. In his last years, he became deaf in the right ear. He joked that he would "listen with one ear but without prejudice". When his right eye was almost blind, he made the self-deprecating remark that he could "see everything with half an eye". In his last year, he suffered from macular degeneration. He said smilingly that "no one inhabits one's eyes". He often joked: "My spirit is not dead."

The organisation and leaders always showed great care and support for Ren Zhongyi in his frequent battles against serious illness in his twilight years. When he was diagnosed with lung cancer, the general office of the central committee designated the expert of the office of health of the central committee to treat him in Guangzhou. While on a state visit, General Secretary Hu Jintao entrusted He Guoqiang, a member of the political bureau and director of the organisation department of the CPC central committee, to see Ren Zhongyi and pass on what the general secretary said: "You are not only the pioneer of reform and opening up in Guangdong but you have also played a vital role in this process throughout the country. I hope you will make a full recovery." He felt gratified at these words and expressed his thanks to the central committee and Comrade Hu Jintao.

In November 1983, Ren Zhongyi was diagnosed with cholecystitis, inflammation of the gallbladder, and was hospitalised in Beijing for the first time. Wu Weiran[1] performed the surgery himself to remove the organ. During surgery, Xi Zhongxun, member of the political bureau of the central committee and secretary of the central committee secretariat, waited in the hospital for information and did not leave until hearing that the operation had been a success. Later, Ren Zhongyi and Wang Xuan paid a special visit to Xi Zhongxun to convey their thanks. The two pioneers of reform developed stronger ties.

When being treated for bladder cancer in Guangzhou hospital on 24 May 2002, Ren Zhongyi was astonished to hear of the death of Xi Zhongxun. With deep sorrow, he immediately asked his son Ren Kelei to deliver his condolences in Beijing. Kelei came to the door of the Xi family, and Xi Zhongxun's daughter, Xi Qiaoqiao, led him to the mourning hall. Kelei was pained to see a portrait of Xi Zhongxun in the middle of the hall, bowed three times before it, firmly held the hands of Xi Jinping standing beside him, and said: "My parents feel deep sorrow for your father's death but they cannot come and pay their respects in person because my father is hospitalised. They asked me to offer you their condolences on their behalf. They often talk about your father, especially when he, on behalf of the central committee, waited in the hospital while my father had his gall bladder removed in 1983 and did not leave until the operation was completed. It moved our whole family very much and we will always remember it. He was a good and compassionate man. May he rest in peace. Please accept my condolences. Xi Jinping nodded his head and tightly held the hands of Ren Kelei.

The description "being alive in spirit, full of courage and strength, fearless and seeing everything with half an eye" truly reflects the life of Ren Zhongyi, the pioneer of reform. His ardent loyalty, profound thought, practical demeanour, wisdom, courage, resolution, charm and great contributions have been bequeathed to the people and subsequent generations.

Chronology of Ren Zhongyi's Life

1914

20 September: born to an ordinary teacher's family in Xixiao village, Liyuantun town (enclave of Guan county, Shandong before 1940), Wei county, Hebei province. His father Ren Yanfo was a middle school teacher in Shandong

1917

Early 1917: mother gave birth to a girl named Ren Yurong

1919

Spring: mother died of black fever

Summer: older sister died of plague

Autumn: father remarried and brought his second wife, Han Qimei, and their son to Heze, Shandong province where he taught

1920

Autumn: stepmother gave birth to a son named Ren Lantian

1921

Autumn: studied at Zhili first model primary school of Tianjin (now Tianjin Zhongying primary school) and was taught by headmaster Liu Baoci, a famous modern educator in Tianjin

1928

Autumn: studied in Hebei first provincial middle school (now Tianjin third middle school), was taught by headmaster Ma Qianli, famous patriotic activist and educator in Tianjin and fostered his patriotism and high aspirations

1931

Autumn: studied at Hebei College of Law and Commerce in Tianjin, was taught by CPC members and famous communist professors such as Zhang Youyu, Yang Xiufeng and Nanhanchen, began to learn about Marxist theories and energetically participated in publicising the anti-Japanese national salvation movement

1934

Autumn: admitted by the department of political economy of the University of China in Beijing, educated by a group of communist professors including Li Da, Wu Chengshi, Huang Songling, Cao Jinghua and Qi Yanming, studied Marxist theory and turned from a patriot into a Marxist

1935

9 December: under the lead of Dong Yuhua, his senior fellow apprentice from the same department, joined the students of schools and universities in Beijing to hold a large-scale demonstration (later known as the 'December 9 movement') to show their opposition to the establishment of the 'Hebei-Chahar political council'

16 December: participated in organising progressive students of the University of China to join the second anti-Japanese demonstration of school and university students in Beijing

1936

21 February: Reactionary military guards besieged the University of China, stormed into the campus and arrested more than 60 students and one professor. He participated in the actions to protect the university. The incident was also called the Snowy February Day incident

24 February: To protest against demands of the reactionary university authorities that students boycotting classes resume classes, he and Yang Yichen took off and hid the university's large bell

28 February: joined the Communist Youth League of China and acted as party branch secretary of University of China, as introduced by Li Quan, a student of Beijing Institute of Political Science and Law

Early June: turned from a league member to a CPC member and acted as commissar in charge of the University of China's party organisation

June: lived in Dequan apartment in Taipu street of Xidan, met a girl student named Wang Xuan in exile from northeast China and living in the same apartment. They later married

13 June: organised progressive students of the University of China to join other students in Beijing to launch a successful demonstration against Japan's decision to increase soldier numbers in north China

Late June: acted as party branch secretary of the University of China

12 December: reorganised progressive students of the University of China to join other students in Beijing to launch a large-scale demonstration to resist Japan and save the nation, which succeeded thanks to his proper direction and rigorous organisation

1937

Late June: acted as secretary of northwest district CPC committee in Beijing

7 July: Lugouqiao incident broke out

29 July: Beijing fell into enemy hands. Organised student party members and vanguards of the liberation of the Chinese nation to evacuate Beijing in groups as instructed by the Beijing municipal CPC committee

10 August: rushed to Jinan with Wang Xuan and administered the membership credentials of many party members in exile from Beijing and Tianjin

Mid-November: returned from Jinan to Beijing with Wang Xuan to administer the membership credentials of the party members remaining in Beijing. The couple went to a studio in Xidan, Beijing to take their wedding photo

Late December: arrived at the office of the eighth route army in Xi'an and got ready to head for Yan'an

1938

January: took office as chief of the organisation section of the political training bureau and commissar in charge of organisation of the CPC general party branch of the 66th division of the Shanxi-Suide army

May: received orders, rushed to Liaocheng, Shandong province, acted as political instructor and member of the general party branch (later also as secretary of the CPC general branch) of Liaocheng political cadre school in northwest Shandong, gave lectures on dialectical materialism and political economy, and compiled teaching materials for *Course on Common Knowledge of Political Economics*

October: acted as secretary general of the headquarters of the third column of the northwest Shandong anti-Japanese guerrillas

16 November: Japanese army captured Liaocheng

26 November: dispatched to act as president of the military and administrative cadre school of the sixth branch of the Shandong column of the eighth route army in Taixi

1939

September: dispatched to serve as deputy director general of south Hebei administrative education office, deputy director general of south Hebei party committee cadre education office and president of the CPC's south Hebei party committee and party school

1941

March: started south Hebei administrative cadre school and acted as principal

1942

March: started south Hebei political school and acted as principal

29 April: 30,000-strong Japanese army launched four-pronged 'iron defence encirclement' of south Hebei-western Shandong resistance base. Ren Zhongyi and Wang Xuan headed the troops of the administrative cadre school to break out of the encirclement with a narrow escape

July: took office as head of the education department of south Hebei administrative office and party committee cadre education office and continued to take charge of the school's overall work

1943

Summer: acted as member of the standing committee of the south Hebei fifth prefectural party committee and commissioner of the south Hebei fifth subarea

May: he and his wife Wang Xuan experienced the most dangerous iron defence encirclement in their life waged by the Japanese army

November: received orders and was transferred to the north China bureau party school of the CPC central committee to learn the rectification of incorrect work styles and act as secretary of the CPC general branch of the rectification school established by south Hebei administrative office in Taiyue

1944

January: transferred to study in the rectification movement in the north China bureau party school in Matian, Zuoquan county, Taihang mountain; soon became the target of 'salvation' and persecuted to extort confessions from him

November: transferred to the north China bureau to be 'deputy editor-in-chief' of Xinhua bookstore

1945

April: ended studying in rectification movement in the party school of the north China bureau, proved innocent, resumed work and served as member of the standing committee of the CPC south Hebei second prefectural party committee and commissioner of the south Hebei second prefectural commissioner's office

15 August: Japan declared unconditional surrender; he and the soldiers and citizens in south Hebei celebrated victory of the Chinese people's war of resistance against Japanese aggression

23 September: collaborated with troops from the Taihang and south Hebei military regions, organised militias and migrant labourers of south Hebei second prefectural commissioner's office to join the battle and captured Xingtai which was occupied by the KMT security corps

25 September: military control commission declared the establishment of Xingtai municipal CPC committee and Xingtai municipal government with Ren Zhongyi as first secretary of the committee and first mayor of the municipal government. Became one of the first mayors nationwide when the CPC seized political power after the war of liberation

October: rushed to northeast China to establish new resistance base together with Wang Xuan and their sons, according to the instructions of superiors

1946

January: acted as deputy mayor and deputy commissioner of Fushun

Late March: acted as a member of Yingkou, Dandong and Dalian prefectural

CPC committees, deputy commissioner and secretary of the party committee of the prefectural commissioner's offices of these three places

1 November: acted as deputy mayor of Dalian

1947

November: served as acting secretary of Dalian municipal CPC committee

1948

January: acted as deputy secretary of Dalian municipal CPC committee and secretary of the leading party group of the municipal government

July: acted as member of Dalian prefectural CPC committee

August: worked as a member of Dalian municipal CPC committee

October: served as secretary general of northeast China government office and Dalian prefectural administrative office and deputy secretary of the party committee

1950

April: took office as director of Dalian district committee clerical office

October: became member and secretary general of Dalian municipal CPC committee

1951

March: became secretary of youth working group of Dalian municipal CPC committee and secretary of the Communist Youth League of Dalian municipal party committee

1952

June: transferred to be member of the standing committee and secretary general of Songjiang provincial party committee

1953

July: transferred to be second secretary of Harbin municipal party committee

1954

July: elected as a member of Heilongjiang provincial party committee

September: attended the first NPC as a representative in Beijing

1955

February: central committee decided to appoint Ren Zhongyi, second secretary of Harbin municipal party committee, to take full charge of the work of Harbin municipal party committee

March: elected as chairman of CPPCC Harbin municipal committee at the first Harbin municipal political consultative conference

1956

April: elected as first secretary of Harbin municipal party committee at the inaugural session of the first Harbin congress of party representatives

July: served as member of Heilongjiang provincial party committee and member of standing committee of Heilongjiang provincial party committee

September: reported to the party and the people at the eighth national congress of the CPC in Beijing as a representative. Harbin transformed from a consumer city to an emerging industrial centre in a couple of years

1957

April: re-elected as chairman of CPPCC Harbin municipal committee at the second Harbin municipal political consultative conference

Late August-mid September: gave personal directions during record flood in Harbin

1958

July: re-elected as first secretary of Harbin municipal party committee at the second Harbin congress of party representatives

September: took post as first political commissar of Harbin selective service board

1959

April: attended second NPC in Beijing as a representative

November: elected for the third time as chairman of CPPCC Harbin municipal committee at the third Harbin municipal political consultative conference

1960

March: acted as member and candidate secretary of Heilongjiang provincial party committee and standing committee member of Heilongjiang provincial party committee

September: acted as first political commissar of Harbin military subarea

October: elected as first secretary of Harbin municipal party committee at the third Harbin congress of party representatives

December: worked as secretary and permanent secretary of the provincial party committee secretariat

1961

July: directed the organisation of the first Harbin summer concert, which has since been held each year except during the Cultural Revolution. It is the longest and most important music festival in China

1962

11 January-7 February: attended the enlarged central work conference, the 7,000-participant conference in Beijing, to deeply reflect on the mistakes in work since the Great Lead Forward campaign

May: elected as chairman of CPPCC Harbin municipal committee for the fourth time at the fourth Harbin municipal political consultative conference

1963

7 February: directed the organisation of the first Harbin ice lantern festival, which has been held every year until now except during the Cultural Revolution. It has become a shining attraction in China and was the earliest, longest-running and largest ice lantern art show in the world

1964

January: elected first secretary of Harbin municipal party committee for the fourth time at the fourth Harbin congress of party representatives. His tenure lasted until February 1967

1965

August: worked as first political commissar of Harbin people's armed forces department. His tenure lasted until June 1968

1966

16 May: the Cultural Revolution broke out

26 August: was criticised and struggled against by rebels for the first time; was collectively criticised and struggled against on more than 2,300 occasions in the following three years but kept his mental strength to resist the ultra-left line

1967

20 January: was imprisoned after rebels usurped the power of Harbin municipal party committee

1970

Autumn: was released from prison and transferred to labour in 'May Seventh cadre school' on Xinfeng farm, Harbin

1972

June: resumed work and acted as deputy director of Heilongjiang provincial revolutionary committee

July: acted as member of the standing committee of Heilongjiang provincial party committee

1973

April: worked as permanent secretary of Heilongjiang provincial party committee and deputy director of Heilongjiang provincial revolutionary committee

August: attended 10th national congress of the CPC in Beijing as a representative

1975

January: attended the fourth NPC in Beijing as a representative

1976

6 October: the CPC central committee overthrew the Gang of Four

12 October: spoke at a meeting for persons in charge of the Heilongjiang prefectural party committee, thoroughly criticising the idealism and metaphysics of the Gang of Four and became one of the first cadres at provincial and ministerial levels to systematically criticise them

1977

9 February: appointed by CPC central committee as second secretary of Liaoning provincial party committee and first deputy director of Liaoning provincial revolutionary committee to take full responsibility for the work in Liaoning

July: explicitly said "practicality is one of the most remarkable characteristics of Marxist philosophical dialectical materialism" at a publicity work conference held by Liaoning provincial party committee. One of the first local high-ranking officials to thoroughly express this view

August: attended the 11th national congress of the CPC as a representative and elected as member of the 11th central committee

1978

March: attended the fifth NPC in Beijing as a representative

30 June: delivered a speech *To Persist in the Basic Viewpoint of Seeking*

Truth from Facts at Liaoning provincial party committee petition work conference

August: published the article *Fundamentally Bringing Order Out of Chaos in Theory* in Theory and Practice magazine, systematically proposed 'three don'ts' to prevent 'two whatevers', put forward 'four musts' to persist in seeking truth from facts, aroused strong reaction in society and was regarded as one of the earliest of the country's top three senior leaders of the provincial party committees to advocate the truth criterion

4 September: worked as first secretary of Liaoning provincial party committee, director of provincial revolutionary committee and first political commissar of the provincial military region

10 November-15 December: attended central work conference, sharply condemned supporters of the 'two whatevers' viewpoint, and advised the central committee to take a clear stand on the issue that 'practice is the sole criterion for testing truth'

18-22 December: attended the historic third plenary session of the 11th central committee of the CPC

December: published *Emancipation of the Mind is the Great Tide of History* in *Red Flag* magazine, which had a great impact in China

1979

17 February: delivered a speech at a three-tier cadre conference held in Changtu county, Liaoning and called on the whole province to 'help some people get rich first'

31 March: presided over Liaoning provincial party committee meeting to rehabilitate Zhang Zhixin cruelly persecuted by the Gang of Four, then confirmed her title of a revolutionary martyr, called on party members and cadres of the whole province to learn from her and attracted nationwide attention

8 August: proposed that the first objective of revolution is to 'change from slaves into masters' and the second is to 'get rid of poverty and become rich' at a rural work conference in Yingkou

20 September-24 October: headed CPC goodwill delegation to Romania and Yugoslavia. After returning home, wrote a report to the central committee from the perspective of absorbing the experiences of other

countries to expedite China's reform and opening up, and the central committee forwarded the report to the whole party

17 November: called on the whole province to conduct a discussion on 'the courage, possibility, methods and support of achieving prosperity' at a Liaoning county party committee conference, which aroused an intense reaction throughout the country

6 December: proposed to 'better understand and apply the principle of integrating planned regulation with market regulation' at a meeting to discuss the objective of socialist production and was the first person to propose the principle of integrating two regulations nationwide

1980

July: was the first nationwide to propose the slogan 'relaxing control over enterprises'

September: supported production contracted to each rural household at the CPC conference for first secretaries of provincial party committees and became one of the few provincial party committee first secretaries to support the reform

31 October-6 November: central leaders including Ye Jianying, Deng Xiaoping, Li Xiannian, Hu Yaobang, Zhao Ziyang, Wan Li, Wei Guoqing, Yao Yilin and Gu Mu met Ren Zhongyi and Liang Lingguang before they headed for Guangdong to take office

9 November: CPC central committee officially appointed Ren Zhongyi as first secretary of Guangdong provincial party committee

18 November: Guangdong provincial party committee held a conference for party members and cadres above the city and provincial levels where Xi Zhongxun announced the notice of the central committee to appoint Ren Zhongyi as first secretary of the Guangdong provincial party committee. In his speech, Ren Zhongyi brought forward the 'three reallys' policy: special policies should be implemented really specially, flexible measures should be adopted really flexibly and Guangdong should really take the first step

10 December: at the standing committee meeting of Guangdong provincial political consultative conference, he stressed his opposition to three 'specials': CPC members should not have privileges, enjoy privileged life or be special

16-25 December: attended central work conference to discuss economic regulation, requested the central committee to stress centralisation, unification and administrative intervention and economic invigoration, and continued support for Guangdong to implement special policies and made it clear the SEZs were not 'concessions' in China and would not impact China's sovereignty

1981

January: proposed the 'three unifys' policy: to unify the adjustment and implementation of the special policies, to unify centralisation and invigoration and to unify drastic curtailment and advancement; explicitly stated his support for production and work contracted to each household in rural areas and brought an end to the debate on contracting in Guangdong

January: acted as first political commissar of Guangdong provincial military region

February: adjusted the leading group of Shenzhen SEZ and appointed Liang Xiang as first secretary of Shenzhen municipal party committee and mayor of Shenzhen

25 February: expressed to Yuan Geng the vigorous support of the provincial party committee for the construction of Shekou industrial park and decided to grant many favourable policies to the park

March: met Zheng Yanchao, graduate of South China Normal University, supported his statement on the private economy and decided to officially name 'individual economy' hiring labour as 'private economy' and make special policies. After that, the private economy of Guangdong prospered

May: at a state council conference on the work of Guangdong and Fujian, proposed the 'three let go more' initiative to direct the overall situation of Guangdong – "to be more open to the outside world, to adopt more flexible internal policies and to delegate more power to the lower levels"

6 June: at the provincial industrial and communications work conference, stressed the industrial and communications system reform and implemented one 'delegate' and two 'integrates': to delegate power to lower levels; to integrate planned regulation and market regulation and integrate economic intervention and political intervention, and introduced the successful experience of contracting in the rural area into industry and commerce

18 August: met representatives of young individual households in Guangzhou and asked the media to publicise and report stories about Rong Zhiren running a snack shop in the city. Rong Zhiren was the first individual household in China to be elected as a representative member of a municipal people's congress. Individual entrepreneurship flourished in Guangdong from then on

October: tried to win central committee approval to nominate Shenzhen as a municipality with independent planning status, upgrade it to be a sub-provincial city and significantly promote the construction of Shenzhen SEZ

27 October: headed a delegation to Hong Kong and met the governor and important figures there

From 29 October: headed a delegation to Macau and met its governor and important figures

1982

11 January: instructed the whole province to rapidly implement the spirit of the emergency notice of the central committee and firmly crack down on economic crimes such as smuggling, illegal peddling, profiteering, embezzlement and bribe-taking

20 January: separately reported the work of Guangdong and the SEZs to Deng Xiaoping on vacation in Guangdong. Deng listened and said: "It proves the policies of the central committee are right. You should persist in implementing the policies if you think they are effective"

11-13 February: headed party and administrative leaders of Guangdong to attend central committee conference on the work of Guangdong and Fujian to discuss the problem of cracking down on smuggling and illegal peddling, and came under huge pressure at the conference

19 February: asked by the central committee to go to Beijing again, strictly criticised for ineffective implementation of the spirit of the central committee and instructed to write a self-criticism letter. The matter was referred to in Guangdong as 'the second report in Beijing'

2 February-6 March: went to Shenzhen three times to bolster and motivate the party and administrative leaders in the SEZ

22 April: approved the provincial party committee to send material of the investigation team of the provincial agricultural committee entitled:

Report on Chen Zhixiong's Contract Operation to the national agricultural commission that affirmed the labour-hiring policy for rich and influential households of specialised contracting in rural areas, which accelerated the development of specialised households in Guangdong

20 May: accepted an interview with a correspondent from *World Economic Herald* and proposed the principle of 'eliminating corruption, not outside influences', which involved avoiding blind rejection of foreign things but consciously eliminating corruption. It became the policy of Guangdong to persist in reform and opening up, which had a profound impact on the whole country

September: attended the 12th national congress of the CPC in Beijing as a representative and was elected as a member of the 12th central committee

14 October: headed many cadres to a dinner at the White Swan hotel to show their support for the first foreign-invested five-star hotel nationwide invested in by Hong Kong patriotic capitalist Henry Fok

2 December: spoke at the fifth session of the fifth NPC and acknowledged that the opening-up process was not excessive but not open enough

1983

February: accompanied Hu Yaobang to inspect Shenzhen SEZ. Hu said: "Guangdong initiated a new situation and perfectly fulfilled the goal of the central committee"

24 February-4 March: the fifth CPC Guangdong provincial people's congress was held in Guangzhou, reviewed and approved the report *Reform, Progress and Open Up a New Situation* written by Ren Zhongyi. Ren was re-elected as first secretary of the provincial party committee

March: approved Guangdong to take the lead in reforming the employment system, promoted the labour contract system for new recruits, broke the iron rice bowl (jobs for life) system and established an employee's pension insurance system

May: approved the provincial party committee and government to deliver to the central committee a report on cracking down on economic crimes such as smuggling and illegal peddling

June: attended the sixth NPC in Beijing as a representative

1984

23-24 May: accompanied Hu Yaobang to inspect Shenzhen SEZ again; Hu Yaobang wrote: "Handling special and new cases with special and new methods, with the stance unchanged"

July: presided over the standing committee meeting of the provincial party committee, decided to issue document No. 31 of Guangdong provincial party committee and granted 10 autonomies to Shenzhen industrial park

22 October-10 November: visited Japan in the capacity of advisor in a delegation headed by Qiao Shi

1985

July: resigned from the posts of first secretary of Guangdong provincial party committee and first political commissar of Guangdong provincial military region having reached the age of 71

16 September: attended the fourth plenary session of the 12th central committee, required not to act as a member of the 12th central committee and won the approval of the plenary session

23 September: attended national party congress and was elected as member of the 12th central advisory commission

23 September: published *Party Discipline to Be Kept Unchanged* in *People's Daily*

1987

September: published *Flexible Persistence in the Four Fundamental Principles* in *Pioneers* magazine and *Nanfang Daily*

October: published interview *Major Breakthroughs in the Theory of Scientific Socialism* in *Guangming Daily*

November: attended the 13th national congress of the CPC in Beijing as an official representative and was elected as member of the 13th central advisory commission

2 December: published interview *Conscious Application of the Law of Value in Economic Construction* in *Yangcheng Evening News*

1988

4 February: published article *Discussion on the Law of Value in the Early Stage of Socialism* in *Economic Daily* and published interview *To*

Emancipate the Mind is to Seek Truth from Facts in *Theory and Practice* magazine

March: attended the seventh NPC in Beijing as a representative

1989

April: published *On Neo-authoritarianism* in *Pioneers* magazine

May: published *Improve, Rectify and Intensify Reform According to the Laws of Economics* in *Resonance* magazine and published joint interview *Discussion on Party Building and Party Publications Work in the New Era* in *Communist Party Member* magazine and *Party Branch Life* magazine

1990

September: published joint interview *Another Talk on Reform and Opening up and Eliminating Corruption, Not Outside Influences* in *Nanfang Daily* and *Yangcheng Evening News* and proposed that internal and external corruption should be eliminated

1991

3 April: published *Reform, Open Up and Focus on Economic Construction* in *Nanfang Daily*

1992

October: attended the 14th national congress of the CPC in Beijing as an official representative

1994

27 December: published interview *To Build a Socialist Economy, It Is Necessary to Pay Attention To and Bring Into Play the Role of 'Two Hands'* in *Yangcheng Evening News*

1996

24 October: published *Cadres Are Not People's 'Bosses'* in *Yangcheng Evening News*

1997

September: attended the 15th national congress of the CPC in Beijing as an official representative

1998

June: published *The Minority Must Obey the Majority* in *Hundred Year Tide* magazine

2 August: published *Poverty Leads to Change and Prosperity Leads to Change* in *Yangcheng Evening News*

October: published *Exploring 'Taking the First Step' in Reform and Opening Up* in *Bimonthly Talks* magazine

1999

8 October: published *On Emancipation of the Mind* in *Yangcheng Evening News*

2000

April: published *On Upholding the Four Fundamental Principles* in *Nanfang Daily* and *Yangcheng Evening News*

July: Guangdong People's Publishing House published three volumes of *Reviews of Ren Zhongyi*: Volume I: *Breaking Through the Suppression — Bringing Order Out of Chaos*; Volume II: *Taking the First Step — Reform and Opening up*; and Volume III: *'Rights and Wrongs' — Politics and Culture*. He published *'Rights and Wrongs' is Seeking Truth from Facts* in Volume III

2002

November: attended the 16th national congress of the CPC in Beijing as an official representative

2005

15 November: passed away in Guangzhou at the age of 92

Notes

Chapter 2

1. The 'September 18' incident refers to the armed aggression in northeast China waged by the Japanese imperialists who assaulted the Chinese army and occupied Shenyang on the night of 18 September 1931

Chapter 3

1. Li Dazhao, born in Leting county, Hebei province, in 1889, was a Chinese proletarian revolutionary, and one of the founders and earliest leaders of the CPC

Chapter 4

1. Lu Xun, formerly called Zhou Shuren, was born in Shaoxing county, Zhejiang province, in 1881. He was, a writer, ideologist and revolutionist
2. The Japanese imperialists forced the government of the Republic of China to set up governing bodies under the control of the Japanese invaders in Hebei, Chahar, Beijing and Tianjin in 1935. They were known collectively as the Hebei-Chahar Political Council

Chapter 14

1. Golden foals indicate good omens and wealth
2. In Chinese fairy tales, the God of longevity is a white-haired old man with a large forehead, indicating a long lifespan, supported by a walking stick and followed by a sika deer and a white crane
3. Sculptures of children on elephants were forged or carved to denote ideals such as wealth, safety and prosperity

Chapter 18

1. The four modernisations refer to China's objective to modernise industry, agriculture, national defence, and science and technology

Epilogue

1. Wu Weiran was born in Changzhou, Jiangsu province, in 1920. He was a famous Chinese surgeon, an executive member of the 19th council of the Chinese Medical Association and a former vice president of Beijing hospital